# Father Fred and the Twelve Steps

*— A Primer for Recovery —*

## Second Edition

**Ambassador Books, Inc.**
Worcester • Massachusetts

Second Printing and Second Edition  2001
Third Printing 2004

ISBN: 0-9646439-8-7
Library of Congress Catalog Card Number: 96-86284

Published in the United States by Ambassador Books, Inc.
91 Prescott Street, Worcester, Massachusetts 01605
(800) 577-0909

Printed in the United States of America.

For current information about all titles from Ambassador Books, visit our website at: www.ambassadorbooks.com

*This book is dedicated
to the memory of
Austin Ripley,
the founder and first director
of Guest House.*

# Contents

# Foreword to the First Edition

This is an unusual book. There may be others like it, but I have not seen them. It has come into being in an unusual way. A couple of winters ago, I was walking my dog Erin at about ten o'clock on a brisk night with a starry sky. Erin, who was almost thirteen years old, was content to walk at a moderate pace, comfortable in her own world as I was comfortable in mine. I was looking at the stars and feeling the cold breeze on my cheeks and I was not thinking about much of anything. Suddenly, a sentence popped into my consciousness. "Tape Father Fred on the Twelve Steps." With that sentence came an understanding that the talks were to be transcribed and published in book form. I cannot with certainty say where that thought originated, but I did not believe then and I do not believe now that it was my idea.

At that time, the prospects of my publishing such a book were remote at best. But when I got home, I telephoned my friend Bill and asked what he thought of the idea. He loved it. I contacted Father Fred and he agreed to give thirteen talks on the Twelve Steps. The talks were taped at Hogan Center on the campus of The College of the Holy Cross in Worcester. Although the talks were not advertised in any way, the room was always filled when Father Fred spoke.

The talk on the Eleventh Step was given twice. The first time, Father Fred was ill. He subsequently was hospitalized. The second time was more than a year later. The talk was taped at the Jesuit Residence at Holy Cross.

There is a Latin phrase, *Res ipsa loquitur* which means "let the thing speak for itself." I am content to do that because I believe this book will more than justify its publication as well as any amount of time that a reader devotes to it.

The book is being published anonymously to conform with the traditions of Alcoholic Anonymous that members remain anonymous at the level of press, radio and television. However, Father Fred is a real Jesuit, and at this writing he is 86 years old.

Readers who are not familiar with the fellowship of AA should know that when Father Fred speaks of "The Big Book" or "The Book," he is referring to *Alcoholics Anonymous* which was first published in 1939. When he speaks of "The Twelve and Twelve" he is referring to *Twelve Steps and Twelve Traditions* which was first published in 1952. Both books are published by Alcoholics Anonymous World Services, Inc.

A number of people were very helpful in the development of this book. So thanks go to Chris for transcribing the talks, Ruth Ann for acting as an intermediary and suggesting that the Eleventh Step be redone, Bill for his support of the idea, Deanna and Kate for their support and proofreading, the Teresian Carmelites of Worcester for formatting the book, Paul Carr for designing the cover, Sister Sandra Nafrie, SND for proofreading, and Paul Parillo for his help in bringing the book through the publishing process.

Of course, our deepest appreciation goes to Father Fred.

Finally, it should be noted, as Father Fred says often in these chapters, that he is giving his own views of the steps. He does not purport to speak for AA.

# Note on the Second Edition

Since its initial publication in 1996, we have been gratified by the many unsolicited compliments we have received on *Father Fred and the Twelve Steps*.

Although we are much larger than we were at the time of the first publication, Ambassador Books is still what is termed a "small press." We do not have extensive resources nor the reach of a large publisher to extensively promote a book. The fact that we are now in a second printing is due to word-of-mouth promotion by readers.

Father Fred died in May of 1999. He would have been ninety years old on All Saints Day of that year. He is buried in the Jesuit Cemetery at Campion Center in Weston, Massachusetts.

To those of us who knew him, Father Fred was a very special man. He loved music, poetry, a "good" steak, and people, especially people who had been affected, one way or another, by alcoholism. He was wise and self-effacing, with a vibrant sense of humor. And he was holy. His holiness had power and authority. It helped to transform the lives of many who met him and many more who read about him in *The Anonymous Disciple*, the novel about Father Fred and Father Jim by Gerard E. Goggins, or who came in contact with him through *Father Fred and the Twelve Steps*.

The tradition of anonymity in Alcoholics Anonymous ends with death. Thus, we can now reveal that Father Fred's full name was Frederick A. Harkins, S.J., and that during his life he was on the faculties of both the College of the Holy Cross, Worcester, Massachusetts, and Boston College.

# Step One

*"We admitted we were powerless over alcohol and that our lives had become unmanageable."*

Thanks a lot for coming. Your being here is a big help to me. Gerry asked me some time ago if I would talk about the steps, one at a time over a period of weeks. I consented to that, although I told him at the time that I think I'm getting a little rusty because I don't get the opportunity to chair meetings the way I used to. That's the way it goes in AA. I'm not complaining about it, but I don't get as many opportunities to talk about these matters. Besides, my memory for names, people, and places is beginning to suffer.

But I'm here with you as a fellow member of AA, a recovering alcoholic—and a very grateful one—willing to do this.

Maybe there is no need to say this, but it's true. What I have to say tonight and on subsequent nights is just my own way of looking at the program. No doubt, there are other ways of putting it that may be better. I may omit important things. Even though at times I talk as though I'm on Mount Olympus, what I'm really doing is just expressing my own convictions.

At the same time I realize that I don't know everything—but I'm doing the best I can, and I'm willing to share my way of looking at the program with you.

I was in my forty-ninth year when I came to Alcoholics Anonymous. I was stationed here at Holy Cross. I've been here since 1955, when I was at the height of my problem with alcohol. I had become a booze fighter during the last few years of my problem drinking, so I got away with it a little longer than I might have if I had been a daily drinker.

In 1959, I had been a priest for twenty years. I had been drinking for close to twenty-five years. I had my first drink when I was almost twenty-five to celebrate the repeal of Prohibition. That's probably before many of you were born. For the next nine years, I drank occasionally. I enjoyed it, and I looked forward to occasions when I would drink. I did not have any serious trouble, and I didn't reach a point of compulsion. If I had a good enough reason during those years I could stop—for awhile anyway. I didn't get into overt trouble, but as I look back at it, the trouble was building up within me.

After about nine years of that kind of drinking, something happened to me. I didn't understand at that time, but I know now that it was then that I crossed the line into compulsive drinking. Something happened to my biochemical makeup that caused me to drink with compulsion. I no longer drank just because I liked it or just because I wanted it or because it seemed like a good thing to do at times. Once I got some alcohol in me, I could not stop. Compulsion. But I didn't know what it was at the time. I thought it was my own weakness. I looked upon my whole problem as a character problem or a moral problem. I thought that I wasn't strong enough or good enough or loyal enough to my God, my religious order, or my family to do what a man ought to do. I just could not control my drinking. I drank compulsively for sixteen years until 1958 when I was forty-nine.

About a year before I came to AA, a Jesuit friend of mine and I went down to an alcohol information center in Worcester. It was presided over by an elderly gentleman who was an old-timer in AA. Francis H. was his name. He greeted us very graciously. I remember we stayed there for an hour or two. He talked to us about the problem of alcoholism, and we tried to listen, but it didn't really hit home. We left that center with an armful of books. We had "The Big Book" and "The Twelve and Twelve," and two or three other books.

During the next year, I read The Big Book, at least the first part of it that deals with what alcoholism is and how the program works. I also read those very important chapters about "Working with Others" and "A Vision for You." I think I knew what the words said. I think if someone had given me a written examination on what I had read, I could have passed it. But I found out later when I arrived in AA that I didn't really know what the words meant; I did not have a clue as to the real meaning of them.

So in March of 1959, after what I hoped was my last bender, I went out to a place in Michigan called Guest House. It was a recovery place for priests with drinking problems. I was very sick inside. I was on the edge of despair and terribly depressed. I despised myself. But there was enough left of me to at least go out there. I wasn't too clear about what kind of place I was going to. I read a little bit about it, but I was so troubled that I didn't get the full import of it. I arrived on the night of March 6th, 1959. It was about an hour's ride from the Metropolitan Airport to the little town of Lake Orion about thirty-five miles north of Detroit.

That night, I met Austin Ripley, the director of Guest House. He was the instrument of recovery for me because he introduced me to AA. They got me something to eat, and then I met Ripley, whom I venerate, in a little library. He talked to me for an hour. It had to be the grace of God that some of the things he said got through to me. I can still hear him as though it was last night. One of the things he said is that if you're an alcoholic and you want to get sober—get well—and you're willing to follow a few simple suggestions a day at a time, you can not only make it, you're a shoe-in. Another thing that he said shocked me. He said if you're an alcoholic and you want to get well, take your will power and throw it out the window. I watched my will power going out the window, and I was aghast. He said what is needed is a desire for sobriety. Later, when I thought of the things he said to me, I realized that I have to have will power. It says in The Big Book that the place for the legitimate use of will power is the suggestions, the steps, the slogans, the suggestions we get from other members—especially from our sponsor. Will power will work there. But I came to learn that my will power against alcohol and other drugs is of no avail. It cannot do the job.

The next morning there were a couple of feet of snow on the ground. I went to the little chapel and said Mass. I stood and looked out a window at a forlorn scene. There was a Christmas decoration buried underneath the snow, and I said to myself—and I wrote it in a note book: "How in the name of God did I ever wind up out here?" I was terribly depressed—a sick alcoholic who did not really know what the problem was.

I was dry for two months before I got to Guest House, and after I was there for four days, I went to my first AA meeting in the area. We all had to go to at least two AA meetings outside the house. I went to meetings in the towns of Pontiac and Rochester. As time went on, I went to other meetings. Sometimes there was a problem with transportation, but we would get to at least two meetings a week. In the house, we got saturated with AA. All kinds of speakers came in—AA people, professional people, doctors, psychiatrists, sociologists. We got a steady teaching about what alcoholism is, and we were introduced right away to the steps.

In that part of the country, the center of the lower peninsula of Michigan, the general greater Detroit area, the typical meeting is a step discussion meeting. Many of the people there carried a copy of "The Little Red Book" with them. I got an awful lot of help from that book in the beginning.

Ripley would gather three or four newcomers together and outline the steps. He gave us some idea of what was in them and what we were going to be asked to do, if we wanted to recover. I had had a lot of trouble—long benders, hospitalizations. I had neglected my duty, and I had a lot of inner suffering. But even after all that trouble, I had difficulty with the First Step. You've heard it before: "Am I really an alcoholic or am I just a problem drinker?" I had that in spades. It troubled me for a few months. I was getting saturated with AA, but I was still troubled with that question. I wondered if I would be okay if my problem—whatever it was—could be solved by a counselor or a psychiatrist. I went to Rip—everybody called him Rip—and told him that I couldn't grasp the notion of being powerless over alcohol. One time I asked him if he thought I should go ahead and do the Fourth Step so that it would help me to get the First Step. He said that might work for some people but it wouldn't work for me. Instead, he gave me a suggestion that was very helpful. He suggested that I take a sheet of paper and a pen or pencil and make an inventory of my drinking—not a Fourth Step inventory of what kind of person am I—but an inventory of what happened to me when I drank.

The first thing that I wrote down on the paper humiliated me. I was so ashamed of it that it took me three days before I could even write it down. I spent a lot of time in my room bent over the paper with a pen in my hand before I could write it down because I felt so demeaned, disgraced, and belittled by it.

I had been stationed in a major seminary, a house of studies. I had a responsible job as a spiritual counselor. I had studied for that. But at the time, I was drinking. One day I was being a smart alec and drinking downtown. I didn't want anyone to notice me when I got back, so I planned to arrive while the community was having supper.

On the way back I was going up this winding, hilly road, and I paused for a while near a stone fence on a hill overlooking a pond. Next thing I knew, I came to my senses in the pond up to my ears, hanging onto a willow branch. It was a muddy pool and I came to slowly. I slithered out, dripping with mud from my ears to my heels, and I made the remainder of my trip back to the house like a beaten cur. I felt it would be safer to sneak in through the side door and that's what I tried to do, but when I opened the door, one of my superiors was standing there. He looked at me and just shook his head in disgust and turned and walked away. I would have felt better if he had belted me one in the jaw. But that contempt, that disgust....

So that was the first thing I wrote down. After I had gotten it down on paper, I was able to write down some more things that I had done or that had happened to me when I was drinking alcohol. By the grace of God, this inventory helped me to see that my drinking was not due to problems. Maybe I started to drink because I had some problems or because of emotional reasons. There might have been a reason why I picked up the drink, but it wasn't the reason why I kept on drinking. It didn't explain the compulsion.

The light began to dawn. This was about compulsion. Compulsive drinking. It's not how much you drink, what kind of stuff you drink, or when you drink, but what happens to you when you start drinking. I could look back over my experiences and see that in those latter years, every time I started to drink it caused trouble. To a great extent it was interior trouble, but it was very painful. I think that one of the things that pained me the most was that I thought it was my own fault. My conscience compared myself with what I ought to be. I would think of all the training I had, the sacraments I received, the ordination to the priesthood that I lived for—that was the high point of my life—and then I would look at what I was doing. It was a terrible burden on my conscience. But at Guest House, I began to see that my drinking was compulsive.

Just for convenience, let me explain the words compulsion and obsession. I think of the word compulsion as something that I do, something that happens in my body. The word obsession means something that happens in my mind. That was the beginning for me. What a revelation to find out that my kind of drinking is rooted in some physiological oddity in my makeup. I'm powerless over alcohol because of that. I can't safely drink a certain amount of alcohol without triggering this biochemical reaction. In Doctor Silkworth's letter in The Big Book, he calls it a phenomenon of craving. It is the body craving for more. As I found out later, it's the mind, too. But, for the time being, I want to concentrate on the body.

There was a doctor who used to come to Guest House and lecture to us on the physiology of alcoholism. He was an old-timer in AA who was sober for eighteen years when I met him. He said a simple thing that registered with me. He said the whole human race is divided into those who can drink and those who cannot. How simple can you get? I'm in that second class. I can't drink in safety. I can drink if I want to. Nobody is holding a gun to my head and forbidding me. It's up to me.

When I tell you that I'm powerless over alcohol, I'm not admitting that these things I used to feel were true. I used to believe that I was a weak character, that I lacked stamina, that I did not know how to love all the way, and that I was not loyal. All these damnable self-accusations. They may be true but they have nothing to do with the problem. If I were the strongest character in the world, if I were the most loyal, the most faithful and loving, and if I had this physiological x-factor that I have—I could not safely take a drink. Will power can't control it. Ordinary prayer won't control it. God could work a miracle. In my faith I believe that. But if God were to remove this x-factor from me or from any alcoholic, in my understanding, it would be a first-class, physical miracle. I learned from pondering the question, "Am I an alcoholic?" that I'm powerless over alcohol. That's what an alcoholic is.

The second part of the step, "Our lives had become unmanageable," applies right down through the whole disease. It covered the Second Step and the Third Step. Things happened to me on the physical level that were a consequence of my physical addiction to alcohol—my compulsive drinking that I could not interrupt and that would go on as long as I was able to drink. I couldn't eat my breakfast. I couldn't sleep. I couldn't show up on time for my job. I had hangovers. I was too sick to do my job. Those are physical things that happened to me.

My thinking was all screwed up. I was obsessed with alcohol. If the thought came to my mind, "Maybe I ought to stop drinking," it terrified me. I started doing funny things. People began wondering, "What's wrong with him?" When it goes far enough, we do things like directing traffic down on Main Street, or we try to clear out a bar room when we're not strong enough to beat anybody. Crazy conduct. It comes under that part of the First Step. That's insanity, but it's not alcoholism. It's the insanity that has happened to an alcoholic.

Then there is the social part. I can't get along with people. I want to have my own way. I'm self-centered. I'm demanding things be done my way. I can't cooperate with people. I start losing jobs. I get isolated. My whole personality is breaking down more and more, and I am doing things that I'm ashamed of. If I am a member of a religion, maybe I stop going to church or start bad-mouthing God, or bad-mouthing my teachers. All those things that happen are not alcoholism. Those are the difficulties that happen to somebody who has this physiological oddity that makes his drinking compulsive.

The Second and Third Step, which we will look at later, will throw more light on the disease. We have a four-fold powerlessness over alcohol—physical, mental, emotional, and spiritual. That's why we have all these disasters.

These difficulties that happen to us in the moral and the religious area are very serious. They need to be straightened out. But after they get straightened out in recovery, we still have the roots of this illness. I am still a person who cannot safely drink. I am not somebody who used to be an alcoholic and is now all recovered. I am an alcoholic. That is another feature of this disease—we do not recover from this physiological x-factor. We recover in other ways, but the only thing we can do about this physiological x-factor is not drink. I believe that this factor keeps deteriorating whether we drink or not. If after a period of dryness or sobriety I picked up a drink, I'm not going to pick up where I left off. It's going to be just as bad as if I had been drinking all that time. My experience convinces me of that. There was never an awfully long time between my benders—five or six months—and every time I went back to drinking it got worse. Finally, before I got help in AA, I didn't want to live. I was "tired of livin' and feared of dyin'." I was loaded with fear. I was afraid to cross the street. I'd look up and down a number of times and then make a mad dash.

The first couple of years in AA in Worcester, I belonged to the Austin Street Group—what a beautiful place that was for an alcoholic. I met a man who had about sixteen years of good sobriety. He was very active in the program, helped a lot of people. Along came a time when some kind of a financial difficulty appeared in his life. He had to take a second job. It kept him away from meetings for about three months, and he picked up a drink. Six hours later he came to, strapped to a bed in a drying out place in New Hampshire. After sixteen years of good sobriety, it just took a few hours.

There was another member, a woman, who I got to know when I was new around Worcester, who wound up in the Worcester City Hospital after nine years of sobriety. Something happened and I guess she started with pills. She wanted me to come up, but it was thirteen days before I was able to get up there. I walked into the room and she was still in the D.T.'s. She was pushing dogs off her bedspread.

I'm sure you know instances like that. This disease is a deadly killer. And I have it. If I were to pick up a drink and start again, it would be like jumping off a ship into the pitch black, thinking, "I'll swim for the shore." Yet, I have no idea whether it's a mile or five miles or one hundred miles. Or it's like jumping off of a tall building and hoping that I'll land safely. That's me. I cannot afford one drink. One drink would trigger my physical compulsion. I cannot afford it. But I can't continually stay away from it on my own, either.

In the beginning when I thought about the fact that I am powerless, I didn't ask God to help me—I asked him to do it for me, to keep me away from the first drink. That did not mean that I didn't do anything myself. I did what I could. As The Book says, I went to meetings, I continued to ask God to keep me away from a drink, I talked with other members, I tried to apply the suggestions to my life in the program. "But you Lord, you and you alone, are the only one who can keep me from the first drink today and tonight." Somewhere in The

Big Book it says that a time will come when the only thing that stands between the alcoholic and the first drink is God.

The Book says the disease is progressive, destructive, and insidious. The derivation of insidious means to waylay somebody, to lie in wait, like a snake lying in a forest, waiting for somebody to come by so it can strike at his heal. An insidious, deadly, destructive, progressive disease. That's part of what I have to remember.

It came hard to admit defeat and to admit powerlessness. It's hard to admit that you can't do something that most of your companions can do. How hard it is. What helped me as I wrestled with this during my first year is the notion of truth. This is the truth about me. I have the physical part of this disease and I am not going to get rid of it.

Anytime a man or a woman welcomes the truth, opens their minds and their hearts and their arms to the truth, it makes them more real. It puts them more in contact with true reality. Thoughts like that help me.

I not only admit but I accept the fact that I cannot safely drink. Acceptance is one of the most important words in the program. When I first began hearing of acceptance, I thought of something passive—like sitting in a chair and somebody tosses a bag of flour in my lap and says, "Accept this." That is a totally wrong view of the meaning of the word. I was a school teacher so this is one of the curses—I go after words—but sometimes, this is very helpful. The word acceptance comes from two words. The main part of it means to take firmly. In fact, it could mean to capture a town. To overcome and capture a town—to seize it, to grip it. And the second part of the word means to bring it into yourself. So if I accepted the fact that I cannot safely drink as a truth about me—I seize it. I am no longer angry about it. I don't feel belittled by it. I don't care what anybody else thinks. This is my life. I grip this and I bring it in and make it a part of me. Acceptance. I no longer fret about it or feel envious of people who can drink. It doesn't keep me awake at night. I don't think I'm a failure because I can't drink and I don't apologize because I'm not a two-fisted man. That's mythology. The real two-fisted man or the strong woman is the one who can face the truth and take hold of the truth and make it one's own.

Acceptance—admitting and accepting. If we accept the truth and admit that we are powerless over alcohol, then we have what The Twelve and Twelve calls the bedrock on which a useful and happy life can be built. It is built on the truth. Built on rock. Like the parable in the Gospel about the man who built his house on sand and the winds and the storms came and washed it away. But the other man built his house on rock, and the winds lashed and the storms came, but it was on a solid foundation, and it stood firm.

That's what happens to us alcoholics when we admit and accept our powerlessness. Powerlessness is a one hundred percent word. I think of a word like penniless. It means this poor fellow doesn't have a penny. He doesn't have a single penny, if you take the word in its exact meaning. Powerless means I don't have any power over drinking alcohol.

One of the things that slowed me up in the beginning in arriving at this knowledge was that I had been a bender drinker. I think I used to think that if I could stay sober for five or six months, that I should be able to do it for the rest of my life. Typical alcoholic thinking. I would say, "Well, the last time that was an accident. That was a fluke. It won't happen again." I remember coming out of a hospital after being dried out, and saying to myself, "Oh, that will never happen again. I'm too smart for that. That was very humiliating, but that won't happen again." But it kept happening. I was being hospitalized a couple of times a year before I got to AA.

Another thing that kept me from seeing the truth was that sometimes when I started to drink, I was able to nip for awhile instead of going completely overboard right away. That is a kind of booze fighting that would allow me to delay the real onset of the deluge. I would think that if I could nip like that for a few days, maybe I wasn't really an alcoholic. I had the illusion of power. I seemed to be able to control it for a few days.

This troubled me for a while until one day another priest who was a recovering alcoholic used a simple illustration that settled it for me. He used the example of two bombs. One has a long fuse and the other has a short fuse. In other words, with an alcoholic like me, it took longer for the flame to reach the dynamite. But the flame reached it. Just as certainly as it reached it with the bomb on the short fuse. The match is touched to the fuse and after a few minutes, "Boom." In both cases, the bomb explodes, it just takes one a little longer. I saw that and recognized it was true of me.

These were thoughts and reflections and decisions that helped me in the beginning to admit and accept the fact that I, Fred H., cannot safely take a drink. No matter what the reason, no matter what the occasion or situation, I cannot do it. Not because I am a weak character, which I may be, but that's not the reason. It's because I have this x-factor, this physiological oddity somewhere in my system that will not tolerate alcohol.

If I say, "Well here goes. I'm going to have a drink to celebrate something Holy. I'm going to celebrate the Pope's birthday. That's a good reason. That ought to enable me—my God any Catholic ought to be able to have a drink for that." I have the drink and a month later I'm in the hospital because I couldn't stop drinking.

That's the second part, Part B, the unmanageability. The troubles we experience are what bring us to the moment of truth. A year and a half before what I hoped was my last bender, I was on the wagon. I was often on the wagon because I was going to recover by myself. I was going to live a healthy life and get back to normal. One bright afternoon I was up on the hill at Holy Cross practicing some golf shots. That's healthy isn't it? That ought to get you into good shape. So I picked up the clubs and the practice balls and started down the hill to go to supper. It was getting close to six o'clock and I got about halfway down the hill and my knees began to buckle. I looked up at the sun, and it looked like a little black berry hanging over my head and I was shaking. I said to myself, "I must do something drastic about this problem."

I had done a lot of things over the years—psychiatry, shock treatments, talking with priests, reading inspirational books, using my religion. I wasn't drunk all the time. I believed in my faith. I wanted to be a priest. Nobody forced me into it. I wanted it, and I had made a lot of good efforts. But nothing continued to work. Maybe I didn't put enough effort into them as I thought I had. But I tried them. Many of them would work for a short while and then collapse. So when I said to myself, "I must do something drastic about my problem," it meant something different, something more than I had ever done before. I think that was the moment of truth for me. I knew I had a huge problem that I couldn't handle and that ordinary means were not good enough for me.

I still went on another bender. It was during that bender that I heard about Guest House. Father Charles, a very dear friend of mine, who died in the program, came to my room and put a brochure in front of me. "Look, why don't you go there?" he asked. I took a quick look and it said "Guest House." All of sudden I said, "Yes." I had been saying no to him for a year. He would come in now and then and say, "You're looking lousy. Why don't you go away for awhile? Get a rest." No. No. I didn't have the courage to move. But this time, by the Grace of God, I said yes.

After that, when I was able to circulate a bit, I ran into some difficulty from three good people who knew me but who did not really support my decision—my doctor, whom I'd been going to for three years, my rector at Holy Cross, who also was a friend of mine, and my former teacher and spiritual father, Father John Ford.

First I went to my doctor and asked him if I should go out to Guest House. He said, "Oh, I don't think you need to." Then he said something very discouraging. "I suppose you'd be all right while you were there." I went back to my rector and told him that at least the doctor did not disapprove of it. Then my rector suggested that I take a plane to Washington and talk with John Ford who was then teaching moral theology at Catholic University.

The very thought of me getting on a plane going to Washington terrified me. I was having trouble crossing the street, but I did go to my room and I got up the gumption to make a long distance telephone call to Catholic University. And by the Grace of God, who picked up the phone but John Ford. I don't know to this day how that happened. He picked up the telephone. And I told him, "The doctor doesn't think I have to go and the rector thinks it's too violent." At first Father Ford demurred, but when he realized that I wanted to go, he made the arrangements for me. I went two months later.

When I got there and they examined me they decided I had arrived there just in time. One of the professional people there said that he did not understand why I hadn't had a heart attack. You see, the three people who knew me so well, my doctor, my rector and my teacher, didn't realize that I was dying inside. I wasn't limping physically, but I was crushed inside. But by the Grace of God, I got out there.

I've kind of rounded out my story now. That's where I first learned about the First Step with reference to me. What Rip used to emphasize at Guest House is that this is a program of action. You do the step. You do the thing that is suggested and then you understand it. I had been talking to priests like myself and academic people. My approach to a problem was to get the best book ever written on a subject, study it, take it apart, and put it back together. That was the way I would master a problem. But AA doesn't work that way. Ripley kept pounding that into us. You do the step. It's experience. By doing it you find out what it means. *Can't just study or read*

So here I am tonight yakking about it to you. I've been trying to do it the way Ripley said since I came to AA, and I want to keep doing it. It's not something I used to do. It's a way of living. If I stop doing it I'm in danger—I'm in trouble.

I know that thousands of other things can be said about the First Step but that's what I have to say tonight. I'm very grateful to you for coming and allowing me to speak.

Thank you.

# Step Two

*"Came to believe that a power greater than ourselves could restore us to sanity."*

Hi everybody, I'm Father Fred, an alcoholic and a member of AA. Thanks for being here. We started last week and I'll briefly recap what we discussed. I was speaking about the steps of the program and about my own understanding of the steps, my own thoughts, my own ideas. We all know that, but I feel a little better if I say it. I'm convinced of what I am saying. I believe it saved my life but at the same time, I know there may be and are other ways of looking at things. Although I may speak very strongly about something, it doesn't mean that I don't believe that you may have another idea. I'm just expressing my own views.

There's another thing that I'd like to mention at the outset. Here again this is my way of looking at it—but it's important to me because I had a lot of trouble with it before I got into AA through a lack of understanding. You know we commonly say that <u>AA is not a religious program, it's</u> a spiritual program. My understanding is that when we say AA is

21

not a religious program, it means that AA is not allied with any organized religion, Catholic or Protestant or Jewish or Mohammedan or whatever. It began that way when Ebby Thatcher, an old drinking companion of Bill W., came to visit Bill one Sunday morning. Bill was still drinking, bottle on the table, and he invited Ebby to have a drink. Ebby was all cleaned up and dressed up, and he was sober. He told Bill he had joined a religious group called the Oxford Movement and that it emphasized what it called the four absolutes. It was a religion, and Ebby was sober. He was probably the first person who carried the message of AA. Subsequently, Bill got sober and he met Dr. Bob and AA started. They discovered after a while that if AA was identified or closely associated with a particular religion then it was possible that people of other religions—alcoholics who needed AA—wouldn't be able to join AA because in order to join it, they would have to give up their religion or do something that contradicted their own religion. So they disassociated AA from the Oxford Movement because that was a religion. AA is religion in the sense that it invites us, recovering alcoholics, to use our own religion as part of our recovery. For example, one of the first suggestions is to ask God to keep us away from the first drink just for the day. That's a religious act. But you don't have to belong to an organized religion to make it. And if you don't have a God, if you don't have a belief, then AA's suggestion is to try to find God or "use mine" or use the group as a Higher Power.

In AA, it is suggested that one of the tools we can use is reliance on God as we understand him. That phrase too, "As we understand him," misleads some people because no human being can possibly understand God. If we have a concept of God as an infinite being, as a super being who has no limits, how are little minds like ours to comprehend him?

What does it mean, "God as we understand him?" To me, it means the God you have come to know through your upbringing. Maybe you got your concept of God from your family or from the school you went to or from the church you attended. Maybe you don't go to church but you read the Bible and you get some idea of God from the Bible. You certainly don't understand him. You don't comprehend him. But you know something about him.

So with that little preamble, I come now to my understanding of the Second Step, "Came to believe that a power greater than ourselves could restore us to sanity."

Where I started in AA, step meetings were commonplace. Most groups might have an open meeting once a month. Every other meeting we would sit around a table and discuss one of the steps.

As I said last week, it was a wonderful revelation that I am powerless over alcohol because of a physiological x-factor in my makeup that makes it impossible for me to drink alcohol with control. When I came to AA pretty badly beaten and down-hearted and almost despairing, I had no concept of alcoholism as a sickness. I thought of it as a moral problem or a character problem. I had really prayed for many years, even when I was drunk. I was puzzled. Why didn't the loving God that I prayed to hear me? Why did he ignore my prayers? Why didn't he, in his mercy, reach down and bail me out of the mess I was in and help me to be a good person? That's what I wanted to be. But it seemed to me that the harder I prayed, the worse I got. That was creating a problem for me, until I came to AA and I began to get the answer in the First Step. I learned that my compulsive drinking was not something that lay within my will power. That was the opening of the program for me.

Now to come to the Second Step. The first five months in AA, I just couldn't get it. It seemed to me that Second Step meetings would usually be a discussion about whether or not there is a God. "If there is a God what kind of a God is he? And what does he think about me?" I had trouble with it not because I didn't believe in God but because I did believe in God. I would ask myself, "If that's all you need—just to believe that there is a God, why didn't it work for me when I prayed?" I knew that I didn't have the answer. But after some months, I went home after a meeting and decided to put this step under a microscope. I sat down at the desk in my room at Guest House and I opened to the Second Step and I stared at the words. "Came to believe that a power greater than ourselves could restore us to sanity." It was the first time I really saw the part about being restored to sanity. It began to open my mind. This step is one sentence. It says we came to believe that a power greater than ourselves could restore us to sanity. I grasped the idea that it's not enough for me to stay away from the first drink. I need to be restored to sanity. I could see that my need is so great and so serious no ordinary power can restore me to health. Doctors, psychiatrists, priests, ministers, rabbis, and AA as a whole can't do it. It's too serious. I did not yet know the full extent of it, but at this time I began to see that this is so, that it calls for a higher power to do something about it. Well I had a higher power. I was one of those fortunate people who had a God I believed in and loved. So I came into the Second Step through the back door. I saw that the step is talking about the disease of alcoholism. It's not giving me a spiritual or religious lecture about believing in God. It's telling me how sick I am. It's saying my problem is so serious that only God can do something about it and restore me to sanity.

Next I studied the concept of sanity. What is sanity? I knew from earlier reading that the word meant wholeness which means health. I thought of a classical saying that most of us have run across: *Mens sana in corpore sano* which means a sane mind in a sane body or a healthy mind in a healthy body, or a whole mind in healthy body. I already had some idea of the healthy body part from the First Step. If I'm an alcoholic, and I am free of alcohol or any other drug, I've got the beginnings of bodily health. Maybe it will take me some time to recover—to get back on a decent diet and to get decent rest and all that. If I have anything wrong with me besides alcoholism, I can see a doctor about it. But the first thing I have to do to recover my sanity is ask God to keep me away from the first drink. I have to do that for one day after another. And, of course, I have to thank him at night.

Then I was left with the question, "What is the mind?" I got a lot of help with this in the Third Chapter in The Big Book, called "More about Alcoholism." It's so important, I often wonder why it isn't talked about more at AA meetings. It gives a few examples of alcoholic thinking. Like the salesman who's been in the program for a good part of a year successfully. He's out on a sales job out in the country and decides to step into a little restaurant to have a sandwich and a glass of milk. He had no thought of drinking before he walked in, but as the waitress puts the glass of milk in front of him he thinks, "I bet if I put a jigger of whiskey in that milk it wouldn't hurt me." This is an insane thought. It's the subtle insanity that comes before the first drink. The chapter also gives the example of the jaywalker. He lands in the hospital time after time because he jaywalked. But each time he gets out, he tries it again. The insane thought, "This time it will be different." Or the fellow who puts his finger in front of a buzz saw and looses the finger—and then he tries another finger and another. This is alcoholic thinking. This is insanity.

I realized with the help of this chapter and the Second Step that the insane conduct of an alcoholic is not alcoholism. It's a product of alcoholism. In my opinion it comes under the second part of the First Step, "Our lives have become unmanageable." My physical life became unmanageable. I couldn't eat my breakfast. I couldn't get up on time. I couldn't go to bed on time. I couldn't show up for my tasks. I was too physically sick and hung over mentally. Because of my alcoholic drinking I couldn't think straight. My thinking became defensive. I tried to justify myself all of the time. I'd say, "Well it's not as bad as it could be. I'm not as bad as he is." Meanwhile, I was hiding my drinking from my companions and I was hiding it from myself. I'd see a bottle and think, "I will have a good swig but before I have a good one, I'll have a couple of little ones." The little ones didn't count, see? That's a lie isn't it? Lying to one's self, and lying to others. To me that is not the mental part of this disease—that's the consequences of alcoholism.

In the last paragraph of Chapter Three, it says the alcoholic is a person who at certain moments "has no effective mental defense against the first drink." I had read that sentence many times, but one time I picked it up and the light went on. I was terrified. In a flash that sentence illuminated for me why in the days before AA I was an unsuccessful booze fighter who would go a few weeks or a few months without drinking and then pick it up again. There were moments of alcoholic thinking when I couldn't stay away from the first drink on my own thinking. At certain moments the alcoholic has no effective defense—that means a working defense—that will save him from picking up the first drink, even though he knows it may kill him. It says at certain moments, it doesn't say every moment.

As I look back on my pre-AA experience with booze fighting I saw there were times during those dry periods when a drink was offered and I came up with reasons for not taking it, and declining a drink at that time gave me strength. But along came this moment of insanity when I could think of the same reasons that had helped me the day before, but they didn't help today. Yesterday they seemed to be printed in heavy black letters in my mind; I couldn't miss them. But this time it was faint, almost illegible pencil marks on tissue paper. I would think, "This time I'll just take one or two. This time it won't hurt me. This time I'll go right back to work. I'll go to dinner." I would con myself time after time, under the spell of this insane thought, and I would pick up the first drink and it would trigger the physical compulsion. Instead of having one or two drinks I would go on a bender. Some benders would last a long time. Two things would be acting on me. One was physical—the compulsion, and one was mental—the obsession. All I could think about was, "How can I keep it going? How can I get another drink? How can I make this last?"

The word sanity in a narrow sense means sane thinking, healthy thinking, but it can be taken in a wider sense to just mean health. Alcoholism is a three-fold disease and our recovery or our sanity is three-fold; it's physical, mental, and spiritual. So first I saw sanity in the narrow sense—I saw it with respect to alcoholic thinking and I saw that I was equally powerless over that insane moment, when I had no effective defense, as I was over alcohol itself. The only power that could save me one day at a time from that thinking was the higher power, the God of my understanding. So, I had two things to ask for. "Dear Lord, please keep me away from the first drink and please save me from alcoholic thinking today."

The wider meaning of sanity includes the body. We'll see later in the Third Step—the third part of the disease. It took me longer to see that, and I'll talk about that next time. But the whole thing is this: I have to rely on God to restore me to full sanity—first to protect me from alcoholic thinking. The word The Book gave us is "delusion," which means a game I play with myself, in my own head. I've used this example before, I hope it doesn't bore some of you, but I have found it very meaningful. The picture is based on something I really encountered. I stepped into a ward at Worcester State Hospital—which I used to visit in my early days doing twelve step work. Right in the middle of the floor, there is a fellow sitting on a three-legged stool. He's dressed in a blue coat with brass buttons and a three cornered hat, and his arms are folded. When somebody walked into the ward, he would become very disturbed because the new entrant to the room had failed to do reverence to him. He's Napoleon. He's convinced he's Napoleon, and anybody in their right senses, if they came before Napoleon, should bow, or make some sign of recognition. Now what is wrong? It's mental, his thinking is not in contact with reality. He is not Napoleon. His name is Billy Smith or something like that and every body knows him, but he doesn't know himself.

So what's the difference between his insanity and mine? When I'm telling myself, as I did before AA on many occasions, "This time it won't hurt me, this time I'll control it." My thinking was not in touch with reality. The reality about me is expressed in the First Step—I'm powerless over alcohol. One part of me is saying, "I can't drink," and the other part is saying, "Sure you can." That's confusion. That's like pouring water and oil together. Is it water or is it oil? God knows what it is! It's real confusion. Two different things are poured together into one container. My head is a container. I've got two different views of reality. One of them is saying, "You can't drink." The other is saying, "Well, maybe this time I can." So although I'm not locked up in Worcester State Hospital, if you were a friend of mine and knew that I'm an alcoholic and you could read my mind and you could see me thinking that way, you would do me a favor if you got me locked up somewhere because in that respect—the way I'm thinking—I'm crazy.

When I read that sentence in Chapter Three, "The alcoholic at certain moments has no effective mental defense against the first drink," and the full meaning of it hit me, I was terrified. I looked up at the bare wall in the room, and I imagined a calendar laid out there, with each month made visible from January to December. I looked at the whole calendar year. I assumed that some of those days were written in red, and I thought those were the days when this kind of alcoholic thinking was going to touch me. It scared the living daylights out of me. And it continued to scare me for a few weeks until finally I heard what AA was saying. Then I realized, "I've got to do it a day at a time. I've got to do it today. I have to ask God to keep me away from the first drink and to save me from alcoholic thinking just for the day. I don't know what's going to happen tomorrow and I can't afford to be projecting into tomorrow or next week or next year. I have to live one day at a time, trusting and relying."

In the Second Chapter of The Twelve and Twelve which discusses the Second Step, there is a precious sentence that says that belief means reliance. It's like the combination of faith and hope. It's believing in a higher power and that this higher power is on our side. It's like putting your arm around a friend and leaning on him and trusting him to get you over a rough spot. A faith that relies. So this faith that relies, I eventually thought, is trusting, believing, and relying on God to restore me to full health with my cooperation. I am not going to do it. What I'm going to do is follow the suggestions: go to meetings, use the slogans, apply the steps, talk with other alcoholics.

The Big Book says this is where we can use our will power. We can do what is suggested. I have no control over alcohol. At certain moments I have no adequate defense against my own alcoholic mind. There is a traitor inside of me. I remember once reading a symbolic poem about a fortress that is built on top of a steep mountain. It is so situated, that a handful of men could defend it against an army. Nevertheless, it falls because there is a traitor inside who opens up a back door to the enemy. That to me is a symbol of my own alcoholic thinking. Of course, that kind of thinking is not present all the time. Although my obsession is relegated to the back of my head and it is not out front bugging me, I believe that my obsession is still there. If I stop going to meetings or stop following suggestions or start doing something that is going to bother me, my peace and my conscience, I believe that in a relatively short time the obsession is going to pop up again in full strength. It's removed from me in the sense that I think of it as being buried about an eighth of an inch under the top of my skull, covered by meetings and my effort to use the program.

*[margin note: Insurance Policy: Afraid not to Keep going, working.]*

Another important thing that I discovered here is the relation of my emotions—my feelings—to my thinking. The word "mind" can be used very narrowly to mean my thinking power. It can be used in a wider sense to mean whatever is inside of me—the way I think and the way I feel. I heard from the beginning about the destructive emotions of resentment and self pity. I heard over and over again that resentment and self pity are the number one and number two killers of the alcoholic.

By this time I was accepting what I was hearing. I had human faith in AA and in the people who were speaking. I believed them, but I used to wonder why resentment is the number one killer of the alcoholic. I finally found it in The Book where it says that resentment cuts off the sunlight of the spirit. The sunlight of the spirit—I take that to mean something like the joy that I feel because I'm beginning to get a little better—the excitement I feel because I'm staying sober, the joy I feel from a union with a group of people who understand me. It is also the light that I'm getting from the God of my understanding if I'm praying to him. It's like a beautiful light that's shining in on my inside and giving me enough joy to enable me to keep going when the going is rough.

Resentment means going over and over again in my memory some hurt that I received or think I received perhaps years go. I relive it. I call it back in my memory and I live through it again. *Re-sentire* is the Latin. It means to feel again. It's experiencing the damn thing over and over. This is usually joined with self pity. To me they're like heads and tails on a coin, whenever I have one I'm liable to have the other. Resentment and self-pity fill my consciousness with anger that is being cultivated and being coddled and built up. It's an anger that's growing and eating away. It cuts off that light. It cuts off anything like spiritual joy, anything like gladness in the power of the God of my understanding and his goodness to me. Especially in the beginning, but at all times, it is a miracle if an alcoholic stays sober. If we are cut off by this light we're receiving day by day because of God's favor and his love for us, after a while we begin to think, "What's the sense of staying sober? I might as well be drunk."

Resentment and self pity are underlined, but there are a whole host of other emotions. One that is mentioned very prominently is fear. One of the chapters says that self-centered fear is the chief activator of our defects of character. That's because in this emotion we are either afraid that we are not going to get something we feel we have to have, or we are going to lose something we think we can't live without. So there are resentment, self-pity, fear, and the other emotions we all know about: loneliness, self-degradation, and low self-esteem. We try to put on a front with other people, but there is something inside of us saying that we're not as good as they are. It says that I'm always less than somebody else. I'm afraid of people. I'm afraid of ridicule. I'm afraid that if I open my mouth I'll say something stupid and people will laugh at me. There's a whole host of emotions like this. We're often told that part of this illness is emotional. You could say it's a four-fold disease. It's physical, it's mental, it's emotional, and it's spiritual. Or you could use the word mental to cover both the mental and the spiritual, because it's used that way sometimes.

So many of us are quite immature when we come into the program. We haven't really grown up emotionally. Doing that is a very painful process. So who will help us to do that? I came to believe that a power greater than ourselves could restore us to physical, mental, emotional, and spiritual health. It's reliance.

I've heard people say that the emotional thing isn't treated in AA, I think that that's up to each one of us. We don't have to go around talking about our feelings twenty-four hours a day, that's not healthy. But here we have the beginning of recovery. In order to recover, I accept and admit the fact the I have these destructive emotions—just as I admit and accept the fact that I have an allergy to alcohol and I have a tendency to alcoholic thinking. I'm childish. I've got some emotions that haven't grown up. If I want to grow up into a mature man or woman, I need to change. I need to grow and that's a very painful process. But I'm not doing it on my own. It's a "we" program. I'm relying on the God of my understanding or a higher power to restore me to health and to being grown up.

Personally, I found that was a tremendous motivation in AA. When I first saw this in myself—I wanted to be a man, to grow up. I didn't want to be a sick, whining little child. And I found that a terrific motivation, to keep going to AA and to go to meetings and get whatever help I could to bring my emotional development up a little closer to my chrono-logical age. I had a friend in my early days in AA, a man who is gone now, but I used to love the way he would introduce himself when he was asked to speak at a meeting. He would give his name, and say I'm an alcoholic and I came to AA because I wanted to be a man. Or one could say I wanted to

*funny but true*

become a woman, a real man, a real woman, not a crying, sobbing, dependent, frightened little child. I used to imagine myself, being so self-centered, that my tombstone would say, "Here lies Father Fred, a child at eighty-five." I couldn't stand that. So I'd say to myself, "Come to a meeting and see if you can grow up a bit."

I have grown a little and I thank God for it. It comes from relying on God, relying on the fellowship, and staying in action. It comes from going to meetings and using my will power where it can be used and trying to apply the slogans and the serenity prayer and the steps to my life. And it comes from associating with other members of Alcoholics Anonymous and sharing with them the strength and the hope. That is really what I'm doing here tonight, and I'm very grateful to you for allowing me to do it, and I'm very grateful to you for listening.

Thank you all.

# Step Three

*"Made a decision to turn our will and our life over to the care of God as we understand him."*

I 'm speaking about the steps, one by one, as I have experienced them, what I think about them, what I think I've learned about them. I know it's only my opinion. I am well aware of that. But I hold to most of it very strongly because it's what saved my life. So we're up to the Third Step tonight.

I had a lot of trouble with the Second Step. It wasn't because I didn't believe in God, it was because I did believe in him. And as I said before, when I would go to the step discussion meetings, very often the discussion would be about whether or not there is a God. That had no meaning for me as far as recovery goes because I always believed in God. I never went very long without praying. Nonetheless, I kept getting sicker and that posed a problem for me. It took about three more months in AA for me to learn that the Second Step is diagnosing me as a person who needs to be restored to sanity. Therefore, I must be sick. It's got to be more than just the drinking problem. I came to see that the sickness was so serious that no ordinary power could restore me, no doctor or minister or priest or rabbi or psychiatrist—not even AA could restore me to health. It had to be a Higher Power that some of us call God, others just call a Higher Power.

AA doesn't dictate to the individual how to think about God. But in the Second Step, I began to open my mind up to the fullness of the sickness. What does health mean? And to what degree and in what areas am I sick? I already discovered from the First Step that I was physically sick. I found out that I have an allergy to alcohol, that I have some kind of a bio-chemical x-factor that makes it impossible for me to drink without compulsion. That is the principle symptom of alcoholism—compulsive drinking. It's not just drinking or too much drinking or drinking at the wrong times, it's drinking under compulsion—I've got to have another one and then another one.

It was the Third Chapter in The Big Book that got me started on the meaning of sanity. It talks about the alcoholic thinking that goes before the first drink. In the last paragraph of that chapter it says, "The alcoholic is a person who at certain moments, not all the time, but at certain moments has no working defense against the first drink." I understood that I was a person who not only cannot drink safely but who cannot continue to stay away from the first drink. I can't drink safely because of my body and the compulsion to keep drinking. I can't continue to stay away from the first drink by my own thinking because somewhere in my alcoholic mind there is a delusion that this time it will be different. It's game playing—conning myself to try it again. This time it will be different. That was a start towards understanding what is meant by sanity. I was one of those people—I've met many in AA—who wouldn't allow myself to have any feelings before AA. I figured that I knew what I ought to do, and I was just supposed to roll up my sleeves and do it, never mind how I felt. I underrated feelings. I ignored them to the best of my ability but they didn't ignore me. I began to learn from the warnings in The Big

Book about resentment and self pity. Those are feelings. They won't get me physically drunk but they'll set me up. They will keep me troubled. They will set me up for this insane thought, "Why don't you have a drink? You're having such a hard time and these people are treating you so badly that you need a drink." Real alcoholic rationalization. Resentments and self-pity, those negative feelings. They can lead me to pick up a drink. They don't make me pick it up but they make it easier for this crazy thought to appear, "Why don't you try it again? You need it." That's alcoholic thinking and, according the Third Chapter in The Big Book, it is so powerful that at certain moments I can't overcome it by any amount of thinking. It doesn't matter how much experience I've had, how many times I've gone on benders, or how many times I've hospitalized myself. It doesn't matter how many books you or I have read. Maybe we've worked in a helping situation, in a hospital—that won't help. There is only one Power that will protect us from this insane thinking at certain moments and that's the Higher Power that I call God.

That was the start. Now, there is more to sanity than just the body and the mind. If you stay away from alcohol, you get a healthy body. You get the beginnings of it anyway. You get a healthy mind if you get some help from a Higher Power against this insane thinking. How about help for these victim destructive emotions? Resentment and self pity are the two chief ones for an alcoholic but look at all the others: loneliness, low self-image, self-depreciation, envy, jealousy of other people, quick anger, comparing one's self to another, regret— "Why don't I have more talent? Why don't I have more attributes? Why am I not more beautiful or handsome? Why am I not a better talker?" Et cetera, et cetera. All those things get us down, and they open the way to this alcoholic thinking. "I've got to have some consolation so give me a drink or a drug." What I'm saying about alcohol, I believe, generally holds for any addiction, whatever it is.

Now I come to what they call the third part of the disease, the spiritual. I had trouble here, too. It was not because

I didn't believe in God. I did believe in him. I heard people at meetings describing the spiritual part of the disease, in a summary way, as a break down of values. They spoke about a breakdown in moral values and growing difficulty with the God of our understanding or with the religion that a person is born into or brought up in by their family. Standards. So I started with the wrong idea of what the Third Step was saying. I thought it was saying to me, "Now that you're not drinking and you see that you're sick and you need help and you're relying on God, why don't you start doing everything perfectly? Why don't you be a saint?" I went along for a few months in the program, going to step discussion meetings, and when I would talk about the Third Step, people would scratch their heads. I couldn't see how far off the mark I was until one night at a step meeting when a big tall fellow named Ron spoke up.

I had given my confused little bit about the Third Step. At the time, we used a little yellow pamphlet with the Twelve Steps in it. There was a page or a page and a half of commentary that was used just to get the discussion going. Ron pointed to the Third Step, and he said to me, "It says the care of God." I took a look at my own pamphlet and I said, "My God, I haven't even been reading this thing correctly." I was reading the Third Step as though it was the same as the Eleventh. The Third Step says, "Made a decision to put our will and our life in the care of God." The Eleventh Step says, "Praying only for knowledge of his will for us and the power to carry it out." Through the intervention of this fellow member—I'm forever grateful to him—all of a sudden I saw the difference. I had been confusing the Third with the Eleventh Step. Let me explain a little better of what I mean. Taking care of his creatures is not exactly the same thing as telling them what to do. The two overlap. They're closely connected, but they are not the same.

As an example, I thought of a mother working in the summer time, preparing lunch. The children are playing outside in the yard. They're noisy as they're playing. Although their mother is concentrating on preparing the meal, part of her is listening. She cares for her children. If there is a sudden pro-tracted silence, she leaves the kitchen and goes out looking for them. She wants to find out if something is wrong, what they are up to, and the kind of trouble they are getting into. She has been caring for them from the beginning. She holds them in her arms, caresses them, loves them, washes their faces, feeds them, teaches them how to dress themselves, teaches them how to walk. She takes care of them all the time. The child who is fortunate enough to have a mother knows this, and the child feels secure. He knows that mother is there and she loves him and cares for him. That's the first thing that the mother does, but then she also does something else. She gives them the little commandments, like, "Don't bring the dog into the house. Don't cross the street without looking. Don't go out on that pond on an orange crate. Be home by six o'clock for supper. Wash your hands before you sit at the table." Those are like the Ten Commandments. That's what she wants these children to do. Taking care of the children is the Third Step. Telling them what to do is the Eleventh Step. When you put the two together, when the child is being cared for by his mother and is striving to be obedient as well as he can, he has peace. But the two things are not the same.

If I look at the wording in the Third Step and I look at what was wrong with me before AA, I discover I was continu-ally taking care of myself and the other people around me. I wasn't aware of it. It wasn't working too well. But without realizing it, I was continually taking care of myself. I was fail-ing. I was getting disappointed. I was getting hurt. But I kept trying it. I didn't realize that I was a little fellow playing God with my own life. I was in my own care. I look at my years of alcoholism, the obsessive compulsion of drinking—I was still doing the same thing. "Don't talk to me about that," I'd say. "I'll take care of myself. I've handled other problems. Just leave me alone. Get lost. Give me another shot at this and I'll take care of it."

Maybe some are old enough to remember the German battleship, the Bismarck, that was overcome in the war by the British navy. It was still firing its guns as it went under water. That's the alcoholic! The self-centered, self-willed alcoholic, he is still firing his guns as he is going under water. "Don't bother me with that stuff. I'll take care of it." That is a brief way for me of remembering what this part of the illness is in me. The Fifth Chapter of The Big Book goes through the Twelve Steps and gives a brief explanation of each step and how it should be used. When it comes to the Third Step, there is something quite different. It takes four pages, sixty to sixty-four—I've got the numbers memorized, I've read them so often—and it describes the third part of the illness. It's a description of what the Third Step is suppose to correct. And it's a description of a self-centered, self-willed person. I want what I want when I want it. I want it now, not tomorrow. I would never say this out loud. I didn't realize it, but I'm a manager, and I'll manage my life, and if you're not careful I'll manage yours too! I'm trying to make the world around me the way it ought to be. How should it be? Well, it should be the way I want it to be. Anybody ought to know that! Because if anybody knows how it ought to be, I do. Isn't it fantastic? But I'm describing me, with the help of those pages. They describe the alcoholic as a person directing a play and telling the other actors where to stand and sit. "Here are your lines. Speak when I give you the signal." He's trying to orchestrate his will and he does it with the best intention. If everybody would do what he wants them to, everybody would be extremely happy and things would run beautifully.

But the other people reject the great director and tell him to get lost. So he gets layers and layers of hurt feelings. He tries so hard to help people, and they tell him to get lost. How mean people can be? How unappreciative of a great soul who wants to make them happy? So we get sicker and sicker. Resentment, self pity, and other emotions are building up in us. That's because we are trying to do something we can't do. We're trying to manage our own lives in all details and the lives of others. We see everything from our own point of view and that is egocentric. There is a sentence in The Big Book which is very important. It says that the misuse of the will is the cause of most of our problems.

So this third part of the sickness is in the will. The first part is in the body, the second part is in the mind and in the emotions. This part is in the will. It isn't a strength of will that's wrong—it's self-will that says it's got to be my way. How well most of us know and understand that. How disappointed and angry we can be because someone we love is drinking and won't listen to us. Or even worse, a son or daughter is in trouble with alcohol or drugs, and God knows what else, and we feel responsible. As a parent we believe we should be able to change this person to get him to do what we know he ought to do. Of course, there's another thing—if we don't do it what are the neighbors going to say about us? "What kind of father is he? He can't even take care of his own son or daughter." They don't have the foggiest notion of the gravity of addiction. So we can at times be subject to their criticism and even their contempt.

That sentence is very important—the misuse of our will. It's not the proper use of our will but the misuse. "I've got to have it my way." One of the hardest parts of the Third Step is to accept one's own self. We have this ideal picture of ourselves in our minds. "What a wonderful character. A really fine person who you would be glad to know." Then I look at what is happening. Why is this fine person in the hospital drying out? Why is it that this fine man couldn't show up to do his job? He's a priest and he couldn't show up to do his job because he was drinking or because he had such a hangover that he couldn't function. The will keeps trying to be that ideal person. We have disappointment after disappointment to the point where many of us reached a state of despair. We despised ourselves. And we beat ourselves up mentally and spiritually. We compared ourselves with people who were doing good jobs and living good lives—people who fit into society, and had good family and friends.

I think the hardest part of the Third Step—made a decision to put our will and our life in the care of God—is to accept the person that I am. I may not have all these wonderful attributes that are in this wonderful painting I have hanging in my head. I have some good points and some weaknesses but that's the real me. As long as I'm fighting with that—I'm refusing to accept the care of God. He gave me my particular makeup with my particular gifts and talents and my particular weaknesses and short comings. If I can't accept that and embrace it, without feeling envious of others or angry with myself or my family or my teachers or God, then I am refusing to accept his care. It is a very essential part of the Third Step. Accepting myself doesn't mean settling for mediocrity. We strive for progress in sobriety and in whatever gifts and talents we have. But we do it under the care of God. We used to have a saying, "We do the leg work and leave the outcome to God."

Here is an example of what I mean. Suppose after being sober in AA for awhile I decide I better go back to school. So I go back to college and I have a difficult year. I find out I'm pretty rusty. I've forgotten how to study and my memory isn't really back yet. I go through a year and I flunk the exam. That's a tough one isn't it? But if I did my best and right now my best wasn't good enough to pass that exam, let me accept this difficulty as coming into my life from a Higher Power, the care of God. So we think, "That's a funny way for a loving God to treat me, to let me flunk an exam." Something more disastrous could have happened, too. That's a problem for all of us. The only answer to that is to pray for deeper faith and trust.

The first phrase in the Third Step is "Made a decision." I make a decision with my will. With the healthy part of my will, I decide I'm going to do something about the sick part of my will. The sick part of my will insists that everything has to go the way I want it to go. I've got to let go of that and if something disappointing happens or I experience a failure, I'm not going to get depressed or angry about it. I'm not going to throw in all my cards. Instead, I'm going to say, "Okay Lord, if that's the way you want to take care of me today, it's okay with me." That's acceptance and if I can do that then I have serenity.

The first part of the Serenity Prayer says, "Grant me the serenity to accept the things I cannot change." But I don't wait for serenity before I try to accept the thing. It works the other way. If I can accept something like the little failure that I mentioned, if I can accept that then I'll have serenity. If I can't accept it, I'll never have serenity. Acceptance is the key word—to accept what comes into my life today that is beyond my power to change, here and now, as something that's allowed by God. Then I have serenity.

There is another wonderful sentence in The Twelve and Twelve and maybe it's in the chapter on the Twelfth Step where it says, "We discover in AA that we don't have to be particularly outstanding personalities to be useful and very happy." The fruit of self acceptance. It's important to understand that acceptance is not always the same as approval. I don't approve of the fact that I flunked. I don't go around bragging about it. I flunked. I wish I hadn't. Maybe the next time I won't, but this time I flunked, and I've got to accept that. That's what was allowed to happen to me today.

The Third Step is about what happens to me during the day. I can divide my daily life into two parts. One is what happens to me today and the other is what I do today. Things like the weather happen to me. The way I happen to be feeling physically happens. Any number of things including the flat tire that I got today, happen to me. Standing behind the Third Step is a belief common to most of us that God, the Higher Power, is running the world and that he knows about everything that happened and everything that is done in our lives. He is like my mother and my father only he's more wonderful than they are. He knows all about me. For example, he knows that I woke up with a headache and that I stubbed my toe on a chair. He knows that I did a little cussing. He knows all about it. If he's all-powerful, why didn't he save me from those things? Why didn't he stop me from having a flat tire? Why didn't he save me from being insulted by a neighbor?

"Made a decision to put my will and my life under the care of God." It's a belief that this is the way God is taking care of me today. He is letting me have these problems so I can learn to deal with them. I can accept the ones I can't change, and I can ask for the courage to change the ones that can be changed. If it is my own fault let me go about changing it with the help of AA and the help of a Higher Power.

I think of God, the Lord, the Higher Power in the Third Step as being like a lifeguard on a beach. I go for a swim about three hundred yards out. I get a cramp and call for help. He comes out for me in this little boat. He's not like a social worker with a questionnaire. He doesn't ask for my name and address and the last time I missed Mass. He doesn't care what kind of a person I am. I could be one of the ten most wanted men, and it doesn't phase him at this state. He has two questions. He says, "Do you want me to pull you in?" My answer is, "Yes." Then he says, "Will you let me do it my way? Will you stop grabbing me and telling me how to do it and let me pull you in?" That helps me. He's not asking me to be a saint. If I were to say to him, "No. On second thought, dear lifeguard, I'm no darn good. Why don't you go save that old gentlemen in the pink bathing suit who's thrashing around. Just let me drown because I'm no good." If I'm crazy enough to say that, he's crazy enough to say, "I don't care. Do you want me to grab you and pull you onto the beach?" After your life is saved if you want to become a better person that's up to you. You've got the Eleventh Step and your own personal religious beliefs to help you become a good person. The first thing is to become alive. You're drowning and God is willing to pull you in if you'll let him. That's not so easy for us self-centered, self-willed alcoholics. I want to be saved but I'd like to be able to say I did it myself. "He gave me a little help, but I did the real job. I'm tough. I don't quit. I really don't need God very much." That's part of this damnable disease, part of the self-centered self-will.

We surrender into the care of the lifeguard, or the God of the Third Step. We surrender our will, the way we want things to be, and our lives. That means my life from day number one, the day I was conceived in my mother's womb, right down to today, I have been in his care. For long periods, I forgot that or I didn't recognize it. But that is where I've been all this time.

There is so much that could be said about the Third Step, but I would like to conclude this talk with an experience I had in my first year in AA. I was a bender drinker, as I told you, and I had many short periods of booze-fighting dryness. I was always afraid because I had the inner awareness that I would drink again. I was troubled with a lot of depression. I was habitually depressed and occasionally I would have an onslaught of deep depression. Sometimes I could tell it was coming two or three days ahead of time. But sometimes it just appeared from out of nowhere, and it got connected with the first drink.

Just before I came to AA when I would get depressed like that, almost every time, it got me back to the first drink. I would go on a bender, and it would make everything worse including the depression. I still don't know which came first. Did I drink because I got depressed or did I get depressed because I knew I was going to drink? It doesn't matter.

I was at Guest House for about five or six months, going to meetings and following suggestions. I had been dry for two months before I went out there so at the time I was dry for a total of seven months. I was in a new situation with new friends. Exciting things were happening, and I went about five months free of depression. All of a sudden, it appeared one evening. At first I panicked because I knew what had happened in the past. I remember saying to myself, "Oh my God, here it goes again; I'm going to blow it again. Where do I go from here, where do I go from Guest House?" Then I remembered that in the last part of the Twelfth Step it says, "We applied these principles in all our affairs." I sat down at my desk with a little piece of paper and I wrote, "X equals *deal c everything* [handwritten marginal note]

depression. My problem now is a part of my alcoholism. X equals just depression." I wrote down the First Step and very briefly, I wrote, "I can't," meaning I can't change this depression, right here and now. I'm powerless over this thing so why don't I stop fighting it? Why don't I admit it, accept it, and then go on. Then I wrote, "But you my God, my Lord, you can." That's the Second Step—Came to believe that a Power greater than ourselves could restore us to health. "I can't do it, Lord, but you who have all power, you can do it. You're available and you will do it for me." That's reliance. "If I do something, if I put this depression in your two hands right now." And that was the Third Step. I would add some words to the Third Step, "If you want me to be depressed, as your way of taking care of me right now, it's all right with me. I'll accept it from you. I won't accept it from anybody else but if that's the way you want to take care of me, right now, let it be that way."

*I can't He can so let him* [handwritten marginal note]

So I had this formula that I discovered and used for myself—"I can't, but you, my Lord, can, and you will if I put myself and my problem—depression—in your two hands right now." I imagined myself lifting this depression out of me and dropping it into the hands of the Lord. I said, "Here you hold it. I can't. I'm sick of it." I can hardly believe it, when I think back, I went all that night and the next day and the next night just walking back and forth in my room with this paper in my hand and repeating these words slowly. I'd walk for a while. I'd sit down for a while. I'd lie down for a while. I'd kneel for a while. It must have been a weekend because I didn't leave my room. I don't remember going to a meal. I was desperate and I went all those hours just saying those words, "I can't, but you can, and you will. If I put this depression in your hands, right now, so here it is Lord, I'm putting it in your hands." I was letting him take care of it but I was doing something. This is important—it's action, I was picking this awful thing up out of me and placing it in his hands.

After a full day and a night that depression left me. I have had other treatments. In the late forties, I was in a psychiatric lockup for a couple of months with shock treatments. It did something to break up the depression but nothing like this. I was amazed when the sky brightened and the depression lifted. I said to myself, "My God, if this will work for my depression it will certainly work for my drinking." It was a very important experience for me.

Later that depression came back, maybe about four more times, but I was ready for it with the same tools. It kept getting shorter and shallower and it finally disappeared many years ago and I haven't had that kind of a depression since. That's not to say that it couldn't appear again. Only God knows that.

These three steps are the most powerful tools ever given to us in AA for many a problem. I've used it on other things in my life and I've suggested it to other people—not necessarily alcoholics, but even people with moral problems. It's a three-pronged attack on any problem and usually it works.

I'll just give you one example and then I'll conclude. I was giving an OA retreat many years ago. I don't know if you're acquainted with Overeaters Anonymous. But from my knowledge of it, over-eating is the closest thing to alcoholism that I've ever seen. The retreat was in a convent and there were a handful of Sisters there. During the retreat one of the Sisters came in and said that although she didn't have that problem, she was tuning in on some of the talks. In fact she had a problem—she couldn't swallow. I made sure she was in touch with a doctor and getting medical attention. When she told me the doctor couldn't find out what was wrong, I suggested these three steps to her to use on the problem, "I can't swallow." Stop fighting it, admit it, accept it. Turn to a Higher Power, to God. "I can't, but you, my Lord, can and you will if I put myself and this swallowing problem in your hands." Less than a week after I left the place I got a glowing letter from her to tell me that it worked. That is just one of many experiences that I've had like that in my years in AA and as a priest.

So we call the first three steps a spiritual foundation. It's not made up of concrete and steel. The foundation is made of our own attitudes, our own thoughts, our own decisions, and we need to renew those decisions, those attitudes every day, to keep that foundation alive within us.

Before I came over here I said, "Well, I have to put my efforts in the care of God and see if the Lord can take care of what ever it is I have to say that might be useful to somebody."

I'm very grateful to you all for coming and for listening.

Thank you.

# Step Four

*"Made a searching and fearless moral inventory of ourselves."*

Good evening everybody. Welcome. I'm Father Fred and I'm an alcoholic. Thanks for coming. As I've said before, what I have to say is my opinion, I'm very much aware of that. No doubt, there are other ways of looking at the steps. But I feel rather firm about my own view because it has to do with my life. That doesn't mean that I will insist that it's the only way of looking at it.

So we've gone through three steps, the first three steps. I guess we all know how important they are. We call them the foundation of sobriety in the program. We're speaking of a foundation, not made out of cement and steel, but out of ways of looking at things—attitudes, thoughts, acceptances, admissions, resolutions. "We admitted we were powerless over alcohol; we came to believe; we made a decision." This is a way of living, and we need to renew this foundation day by day—to keep it alive and keep it significant in our lives as a sure foundation for our continued recovery in the program.

I also spoke of the second part of the First Step, "Our lives became unmanageable," as applying to the first three steps. Because of my alcoholic drinking, my life became unmanageable physically. I couldn't eat, couldn't sleep, couldn't do my job, and I failed people. Those consequences were not alcoholism; they were the consequences of the fact that I was trying to drink when I can't drink. With the Second Step we focus on the mental and emotional part of the illness, the crazy thinking which most of us went through when we were drinking alcoholicly. You know, the crazy things, like directing traffic at Times Square or driving your car one hundred miles an hour down Main Street, getting into fights, insulting your friends. That crazy conduct pertains to "our lives becoming unmanageable." I don't mean that it isn't important. One of the important things about it, for us, is it helped to drive us into AA.

As I often do, I thought of John the Indian the other day, God rest him. I remember the saying of his, "It's not somebody else's suffering that gets us into AA; it's our own." So my suffering, like yours, was physical. I couldn't eat. I couldn't sleep. It was mental. I couldn't think straight. I was doing things that I never would have done if I weren't drinking. I was playing God and being a self-centered, self-willed alcoholic. I had difficulties, among other things, with my neighbor. As The Big Book in Chapter 5, pages sixty through sixty-four, describes in great detail, this almost spontaneous effort on the part of an alcoholic like me to be a manager and to direct other people's lives is resented by the other people. It creates a distance between myself and my friends and associates. It makes communication extremely difficult, if not impossible. You can't cooperate with others in a task because of this alcoholic tendency to say, "I know the best way to do this." All of those things are consequences of my drinking. They are important, but they are not the disease. They are consequences of the disease. For example, a very important part of the consequences of the disease is the way a person loses his sense of values and does things he would never do in his right mind. Perhaps the person has a lot of trouble with the God he was taught about and with his church. All those things are consequences. They are not the disease of alcoholism. I don't mean they are not frightening. They're awful, and they have to be taken care of.

But I'm looking now at this situation—I come into AA and I have gotten sober. I'm living the first three steps. I believe that once I put those three steps to work in my life, I'm doing something about all the different aspects of my illness— the physical, mental, emotional, and spiritual. Especially through the Third Step, I begin to find out what it means to be sober. Now, I'm not just dry, I'm sober. I'm able to eat my breakfast. I'm able to show up for work. I'm not getting arrested for crazy conduct downtown. I'm not crying on somebody's shoulder, like a crying alcoholic, and I suddenly realize, through this program, that I'm not God—I'm not the boss and—as one old-timer says, "I resign as the manager of the universe." All these troubles begin to disappear. There have been some cases where they disappear almost completely. But the question is, "What am I left with?" I think that what I'm left with is the disease of alcoholism. We hear over and over it's an incurable disease, that the price of recovery is eternal vigilance. We have to pay the price. We need to go to meetings, we need to follow the suggestions, read the books, share with other alcoholics. We are no longer in those other kinds of trouble. We may even be seeking to help people to reach a state of peace with their God. We are not fighting with the God of our religion anymore. So what is it that threatens us? It's the mental part of the disease plus the physical compulsion that is still there, even though one isn't drinking. It's the emotional immaturity, the tendency to be resentful or self-pitying and so forth, that opens the door and makes it easier for this insane delusion to appear in my mind, "Why don't I have a drink?"

Even though I've done my best to make a decision to get out of the driver's seat and to put my will and my life in the care of God, I've got this deep-seated tendency to take it back. It happens very easily if somebody crosses me up. It can be some stupid little argument about a triviality, but it is not trivial to me—"This guy contradicted me." I think you know what I mean. That is dangerous and that's a part of the disease, that's alcoholism. So that's what I meant to say. I didn't mean to belittle these terrible sufferings that come as a consequence of our drinking.

After some months in AA, maybe a half-year, more or less, when we've gotten a decent understanding of the Third Step and when we put it to work in our lives—even imperfectly—it changes our lives. I remember how I could even notice the difference in myself. I began to relax. Up to that point, I was strung out—I had this deadly disease that I had to overcome. But when I reached the point that I understood God was going to do it, and I put it in his two hands, I could relax. As I often heard later on in AA, especially around Worcester and Austin Street, we do the leg work and we leave the outcome to God. When I began to rely on God to save me from alcoholic thinking, in addition to relying on him to keep me away from a drink for a day, it changed my life. I began to grow up.

I reached a point that in addition to this foundation—to what I would call an initial sobriety—I needed to change. If I remained the same sort of person I was before I came to AA—when I was drinking and even before I started to drink—if I stayed the same and I didn't do something about changing, I was in danger of going back to alcohol. It's not a certainty; it's a danger and we see and hear about it often if we go to AA.

How does that change happen?

The Fourth Step, "Made a searching and fearless moral inventory of ourselves." I didn't know whether it frightened me or whether I was having honest difficulties by asking, "What good will it do?" There were two things that brought me to the point were I decided for myself that I was going to do a Fourth Step. The first one was that the people who wrote The Big Book said that they tried to find an easier way and they found out that half-way measures availed them nothing. And I read explicitly that without this thorough inventory, sobriety, if anything, is precarious. It's shaky. It doesn't say that necessarily I will drink or not drink, but it's shaky.

I look upon The Big Book as a history book. It's not a book of theory. It's not some clergyman or doctor or expert theorizing about alcoholism. It's a story of what happened to the first hundred or so members in AA. After a couple of years, they paused and said, "What did we do to reach this point of sobriety where we are now?" That's why, in my opinion, the Twelve Steps in The Big Book are written in the past tense. They said, "Well here's what we did. First we admitted we were powerless over alcohol, then we came to believe that a power greater than ourselves could restore us to sanity. Then we made a decision to turn our will and our life over to the care of God as we understand him, and then we made this fearless, searching moral inventory of ourselves." And I believe I'm one of these people. Why, I don't know. But I'm like them. I have the same kind of illness or disease. And if they had to do a Fourth Step, I've got to do it.

I made my decision first of all on the basis of their authority—not their authority to give me orders but the authority that came from their experience. This is what happened, this is the way they found it to be. So I said to myself, "I'm one of them. I've got to do what they did."

I had one additional help. It was my sponsor. Every now and then, he would tap me on the shoulder and he would say, "Don't you think it's time you began?" He didn't bug me too much except every now and then.

Those were my motives. I didn't at that moment understand the purpose and the value of the Fourth Step the way I do now. So it was kind of a following of authority of leaders. That is one type of faith I'm talking about—human faith, which I think is extremely important in our program—to believe what the old-timers—the people who went ahead of us—tell us. What The Big Book says is a wealth of experience, not a theory. So I finally decided, "Yes, I'm going to do it."

Then my next question was, "How am I going to do it? What is the method?" Many people get hung up on that, and

I can sympathize with them. I first tried the method described in The Big Book where the individual takes a topic like society and goes through his whole life in relation to that topic. Then he takes another topic, money for example, and he runs through his whole life on that—and so forth through a variety of topics. And I said to myself, "If I try it that way, I'll go mad. I just know I can't do it that way."

Was that an honest judgment of mine? I don't know. It was a judgment I made. Weeks went by and I was still going around wondering how I was going to do it. I was still determined to do it, but I hadn't started yet! Finally, a man who was counseling me helped me. He said, "Why don't you divide your life into parts, sections, and then sit down with each section of your life and just jot down what you can remember about that period of your life. So I started with my ordination to the priesthood. At that time, I was a little over twenty-nine years old, and after my ordination I lived in the same house for three years.

I sat down twice a week to write. I had the time available. I realize that not everybody would have that available time. But I was fortunate. I was in a recovery place for priests, and my job was to do what was required to get well. So twice a week, for an hour and a half or so, I would sit down at my desk with paper and pencil and I would concentrate on those three years.

I had already made up my mind that I better not decide what kind of a person I am before I started writing. I knew some of my defects. I knew them well because I used to go to sacramental confession as a Catholic. That's different, of course, from this inventory, and I may speak about it later. I was used to doing some kind of examination. So I said, "I better not tailor this thing. I'm just going to write down the facts." You know, like Friday, "The facts ma'am, just the facts." I sat down, and if anything came to mind that happened during those three years, whether it was something that I did or something that was done to me, I would jot it down. I would also jot down how I felt about those things.

Frequently, I would not have to write out a paragraph to describe the thing. If it was something that happened only once or twice, I might have to describe it. But if it was the type of thing that was habitual, it was enough to put a word down or a phrase. The way I looked at it was that I wanted to get enough words on paper, enough phrases and sentences so that I could pick up that paper at a later date and use that to help me tell another man exactly what was going on in my life during those three years. That was the simple way that I looked at it.

I didn't rack my brain at the time over whether something was a sin or a defect or a weakness or a character trait. If it was about me, I put it down. This was my inventory.

I did it patiently. Some days when I sat at my desk, not a thought would come to me. I knew that was going to happen now and then. I had to resolve that when it happened, I would not get mad about it or get discouraged. I decided I would just sit there. Something was going on even if it was subconscious. So I thought that the next time I sat down, a couple of days later for another session, that maybe it would come then. That's the way it worked out.

Following that three-year period, after I was ordained, I was assigned to another house that I lived in for ten months. I took that ten-month period and I did the same thing with it. I wrote about the periods of my life according to where I lived or what school or what college or what seminary I was at, until I brought it down to the present day in AA. Then, still following this man's advice, I went back to where I began the inventory—my ordination to the priesthood—and I worked backwards. I wrote about the three years of study just prior to ordination, then two years before that. I taught at Holy Cross for two years before I was ordained—ages ago— back in the thirties. I took that two-year period and did the same thing with it, and then I went back to an earlier study period of three years, and so on. I was amazed how far back I got into my childhood with a few little things. I think that process took me about ten months.

I got a sheaf of paper. I used to make duplicate copies. I would bring the two papers to this counselor who was helping me. I would give him one paper and I'd keep the other and we would go through my story. He had a scientific name for it, but that's what we did. That was a big help to me, to gather together the facts—what went on in my life.

I knew that there were some things, maybe many things, that were in my story that were of no interest to him. He would just brush them aside. He could not see how he could use them in what he was doing. When I finished with him, I sat down again and I added the things that were important to me. I had a pretty good sheaf of papers and I had that extra help that helped me to focus on writing out my Fourth Step—but I feel sure I would have done it anyway.

Incidentally, before I started working with that man, I had been around Guest House and I read about AA for about a year. I had read The Big Book. I didn't really know what it meant, but I had read it. When I was told that it would be helpful to meet with this man, I spent about three weeks debating with myself the question, "If I deal with this man, how will I look upon myself? Will I look upon myself as an AA member who is also getting help from a professional or will I look upon myself as a client of a professional counselor who also goes to AA. Thanks be to God, I knew enough that I finally decided, "I'm an AA member, that's who I am. I'll go to him for whatever help he can give me but if he ever contradicts AA, I'll just ignore him." He never did contradict AA, but that was my attitude and I think it helped me because it was necessary for me to keep my alcoholism and my AA program first and not to allow anything to interfere with that.

But back to the Fourth Step. I took some time to add to this sheaf of papers things that were of no interest to this psychologist, but they certainly were matters of life and death to me. As we read in The Big Book and we hear often, it could be some seemingly small thing that can do a lot of damage to us. I didn't want that to happen.

Now the word moral—we say "a moral inventory." If I were to take that word in the strict sense, I would be dealing with what is good and what is bad, what's virtuous and what's sinful. I would be dealing with what are my virtues and what are my vices; what sins do I tend to commit. That's the strict meaning of it. What's my relationship to my conscience. But in looking at that step in the light of The Big Book and AA experience, I believe the word moral has a much wider meaning than that. My inventory will include things that were wrong in the sight of God. The bulk of it were things about me that were not sins. They were parts of my sickness, my emotional sickness, my self-centered, self-willed sickness, and my crazy thinking. Just to give you an example, I think almost every alcoholic that I've met has suffered sometime from anxiety. Well, I did too, and that was part of my Fourth Step—I had a lot of anxiety, but anxiety is not something that I'm doing. I'm not deliberately violating my conscience or offending God when I feel anxious. I can't help it. It's an emotional weakness or difficulty, a distortion. God knows where it came from. That's just one example. I wouldn't go to confession to a priest in the Catholic Church and say, "Father, since my last confession I've been anxious three times." He'd say, "Is that so. It's not a sin." But my anxiety may have played a large part in making it easy and giving me excuses to pick up a drink.

Another example would be nervousness. A fellow is nervous in public. He shakes. He's self conscious. If he thinks that people are looking at him he goes through agony. Is that moral in the strict sense? Of course not. But it's moral in the wide sense because it's a part of his makeup. You can think of many other emotional traits, tendencies like that.

That's my understanding of the subject matter of the Fourth Step. It's not just my sins but all these other things in me—weaknesses or emotional distortions or emotional habits that made my life miserable. They make it harder on me to enjoy life, to enjoy sobriety. I get them all down on paper.

I think of the two adjectives in this step, "searching and fearless." To my way of thinking, they're perfectly chosen.

Perfectly. First of all "searching." At times when I was writing down this fascinating story of my life, it was like writing down warmed over beans. It was even putting me to sleep. But The Book said, "Do it. Do it thoroughly and be searching." So at times I had to sort of get geared up to be searching. "Now don't goof off here. Do this thoroughly. Sure it's boring. Sure you're sick and tired of it. Put it down. Do you want to get well? Write it down." And that's tough because this is hard work. It's hard work to make this complete thorough inventory—searching.

Then the other one—"fearless." That's a big one, too. The way I felt in the beginning was that I knew enough bad stuff about myself to make me want to commit suicide at times. "Why should I dig up something else? Why shouldn't I let sleeping dogs lie?" It's a temptation. "I'm all right now, anyway. I'm going to meetings. The heck with that." What a temptation. So I'd get back to the testimony of The Big Book—"without a searching, fearless, moral inventory, sobriety—if any—will be precarious." Do I want precarious sobriety? Do I want to go this far with recovery and then hang back? No, I want the whole thing. Just as I did when I was drinking, I wanted the whole bottle. I want the whole program. Those two words are perfectly chosen for people like us. "Searching and fearless."

It's recommended to write the Fourth Step down. It's not a commandment of course. It's suggested and its value is that when we have a part of it written down, we don't have to try to remember it anymore. It's down there on paper. Now our mind is free to explore some other area of our life. So that was some of my experience with the Fourth Step. After I had written down the Fourth Step to the best of my ability, I felt better. I had accomplished something. I remembered having read some years previously when I was in my troubles that if we make up our minds to go into action, to do something, we begin to feel better. So I began to feel better and at the same time to feel pretty awful when I looked at these pages all about me. It's all about me. I also heard and I believe this, that through such an inventory I come to know myself better. I come to a better knowledge of my strong points and my weak points. I come to a better knowledge of what I need to develop, what is good in me, what needs to be developed, and what's weak or bad, or sick in me to be worked on through the program.

In the case of sin and real guilt, and this is my own faith, real guilt exists for me when knowingly and willingly I have done something that I know is wrong. It doesn't coincide with my conscience and it doesn't please God. Real guilt, as I understand it, is a condition, a relationship. It's not only a feeling. It's a relationship between me and God. If I'm really guilty, say of robbing a bank, God could point at me and say, "Now, you are the man who robbed that bank," and I would have to say, "Yes, Lord, I am." That's real guilt. I may feel it more or less deeply, but it isn't the feeling that makes it guilt. It's that real situation—the relationship between me and the God of my understanding. And the only one who can forgive that is God. AA can't forgive real guilt. AA is not a religion, it's a therapy. AA suggests that we turn to a Higher Power, or a God as we understand him. AA leaves that to the individual. We settle that question with God. But we have a lot of other guilty feelings that are not always grounded in a real offense. Because some of us tend to feel guilty before anything happens at all. If something goes wrong we start looking around—"What did I do?" It's fantastic, isn't it? In those awful days, when I could read, I would pick up a newspaper, and read about some accident over in China, and I would feel somewhat guilty. "I should have been there to stop that." Now there's a little bit of ego in there, too. That's guilt mixed up with this great big alcoholic ego. The manager. God's first assistant.

So what AA can help us with is that falsehood, that exaggerated guilt and it does this through the program. I think that would come under "Came to believe that a Power greater than ourselves could restore us to sanity," to health of the body, to health of the mind—thinking—to health of the emotions. If I'm walking around feeling guilty for the conduct of the Chinese government or something like that—I'm sick. It's real; it happens to us. So this program, especially this step, relies on God to restore us to emotional balance and health. But that's a big problem for us—the guilt feelings. By facing whatever the real guilt is and bringing it to the God of our understanding, we can come to terms with it and seek forgiveness.

Another example of what we call excessive guilt or neurotic guilt, is that some people can never believe that they've been forgiven. If I did you some injury, let's say I insulted you, and two days later I thought it over and I felt sorry for it. I went to you and I apologized and I asked you to forgive me and you said to me, "Yes, I forgive you from the bottom of my heart, let it be forgotten." Then I meet you the next week and I say "Remember that thing that I did to you? Did you really forgive me?" And you say, "Yes" and I keep doing this for the next twenty years. I meet you once a week. Am I exaggerating? Maybe a little bit. But there are people like that. They cannot accept forgiveness. So we're back to that tremendous word "acceptance" and taking a fellow creature or taking God, the God of your understanding at his word, and reaching out and accepting forgiveness and being willing to be forgiven. That's quite a bit of growth in emotions and in the spirit. It's been a long time since I did the Fourth Step, and it was really work. But I have never looked back in my experience in AA and said to myself, "Gee, I'm sorry I spent so much time on it." I just thank the God of my understanding that he enabled me to do it and to do it as thoroughly as I could.

That word "thorough" is underlined and emphasized in AA. One of the reasons as we all know, but I'll tell you again, is that if we leave something out because we are afraid to express it even to ourselves—we don't dare acknowledge it and admit it, in our consciousness—it's just too horrible—that's not going to disappear. That remains down somewhere within us and I don't say that it necessarily will, but it can cause trouble. It can be like some kind of a germ that's eating away at our recovery and our health.

That impressed me very much in The Big Book—that plea for thoroughness. So that's been my experience with the Fourth Step. Now, there are other ways of doing it, like using some of these questionnaires. I've seen a few of them. I remember listening to Fifth Steps of people who used the scheme developed by Eddie O., and I thought that covered the ground very well. Some people can use one of those schemes to do it. But this is the main thing, if you haven't done it yet—if you're standing on the bank of a stream and you're dipping your big toe in and pulling it out—take the plunge. Get a notebook and a pen or a pencil and sit down and write at the top of Page One, "My name is Fred" or John or whatever it is. The Book says it's important to make a start. And this is a suggestion, dwell on these assertions in The Big Book and see if it doesn't help you to get started.

I'll close with what I started with—The Big Book says that without a thorough inventory of self, sobriety, if any, will be precarious.

Thank you all for listening.

# Step Five

*"We admitted to God, to ourselves and to another human being, the exact nature or our wrongs."*

I know that many of you, if not all of you, are thinking of Old Tony, who died recently. He is going to be buried tomorrow. There's a Mass at St. Casimir's at ten A.M. I just heard tonight that he was discovered in his room by a sister and a brother. He was sitting before a television set with The Big Book in his lap. It was opened to page sixty-four. We talked about those pages in the Third Step—he was just about finished reading about the Third Step. This wonderful gentleman, recovered alcoholic, who built his life on AA which was so dear to him. He continually pondered it. He had a wonderful memory, and he loved to recall people he had known and what they had said—little bits of wisdom he used to share. After these many years of AA life and sharing with others, he has gone to his reward. These are just a few words of tribute to a great AA man.

We're up to the Fifth Step tonight. As you know, I'm just speaking my own thoughts about it, what I believe about it. I know that it's only one man's opinion. But that opinion is important to me as yours is to you. For it saved my life. In this part of the program, the inventory part, we have achieved some realization of sobriety with the first Three Steps, and we come to some degree of understanding what it means to be sober, rather than to be just dry. The program suggests to us that we do something about ourselves to change in a positive direction. If we don't change, if we remain the same kind of people we were before the program, there is danger of us, after a while, getting tired of sobriety and lapsing back to alcoholism. When I first looked at the Fourth and the Fifth Steps, my reaction to them was negative. "If I do that as thoroughly as they say, won't that depress me? Won't that make me feel worse than I already feel?" Maybe you felt that way. I found out by my experience the truth of what had been told to me by my sponsor. By doing these steps that look so negative, the result is joy. It's a paradox. That's what happens to those who face these difficult Steps and do them to the best of their ability. It doesn't depress them; it lifts them up. It means the beginning of an interior change. It's hard to define or describe, but when we do it we get some understanding of what it means. In order to approach the Fourth and the Fifth Steps, I needed to have the Third Step more or less secure in my life. I needed this part of it—probably the most difficult part of the Third Step—to accept my own self.

Accepting doesn't necessarily mean approving. There were things in my life before AA that I cannot approve, and I don't even intend to try to. But I have to accept them. I have to accept the fact that they did happen. I have to be willing to accept that they happened while under the care of a Higher Power. To me, that was God. I know that maybe some people have difficulty here, but in my own case I didn't have that difficulty. I believe that "Made a decision to put my will and my life in the care of God" means my whole life, from the very beginning in the womb of my mother up to the present time, and whatever remains of my life. I believe that the God of my understanding knew all about my life. We are in his care. He is the caretaker, the one who knows all about me and wants the best for me and watches over me. He doesn't abandon me even when I think I've turned my back on him. That's an understanding that some have about the Higher Power and it is mine. Whatever it was that happened in my life, God as I understand him, knew and knows all about it. He didn't turn me off. Instead, he called me into this program, and he gave me the willingness and the daily help and all you people to help me to turn things around and to begin to be sober and to live a life of sobriety.

I think that we really need some degree of self-acceptance to write down the Fourth Step. We hear people say, "There was something in my life that I swore I would never divulge to anybody. I'd never write it down. I'd never tell another person. I thought it was so bad." We hear that often enough. That's where we need this kind of self acceptance. "Yes, that wasn't too good. That was pretty bad. But it happened and God didn't strike me dead when it happened. Instead he's trying to lift me up. He's willing to heal me and to forgive me." I think this kind of attitude is needed before I tackle this task of writing down on paper an account of my life.

The Fourth Step is not a club that I'm putting together to beat myself with. I'm not doing the Fourth Step so I can pick up these papers and say, "You damn this, that, and the other," and whack myself over the head with it and go around moaning and groaning. No, it's to find out who I am and where I am. Who am I? Where am I? It's all about me. What could be more interesting than something that's all about me. Not in order to crucify myself but to find out where I go from here. Years ago I had a brilliant idea. It's probably the only brilliant idea I've ever had in my life. It dawned on me that in order to go some place I have to start from where I am—not from where I think I am, not from where I would like to be—but from exactly where I am. What a brilliant idea that is. And I've done it. So there's hope for all of us.

One more preliminary idea on the Fourth Step—I found myself starting the Fourth Step and my mind would project into the future—the Fifth Step. I found myself shaking and worrying about what was going to happen when I told this to another man. "What's he going to think of me? Will he stay there or will he get up and walk away?" I developed a technique for dealing with those fears about the Fifth Step. I tell myself, "Maybe I'll never do the Fifth Step. The heck with the Fifth Step. But I can do the Fourth Step. If I do it and get a better picture of myself, that will be progress. Then later on, maybe, I might do the Fifth." I did my best to keep them separated so that I would be free to concentrate on the Fourth Step and not have my memory blocked or troubled by thoughts about what it was going to be like to say this to another person. I found that very helpful.

I would try to get down on paper enough words or signs or marks so that I could use these papers to help me tell another person all I knew about me to the best of my ability. After I had the stuff down on the paper then I could look it over and say, "Do I find any trends? Do I find any habitual ways of acting here?" I did that for awhile to try to pick out whatever patterns I could find in my stories. To tell you the truth, I didn't learn an awful lot about myself that I didn't already know, but I learned something. And at least I did this step.

Early in the program reading The Big Book, I came across a sentence that said, "The alcoholic needs to be restored to the human race." When I first read it, I was tempted to laugh. It sounded like some kind of high flown rhetoric. But as I went along in the program I discovered that it's the exact truth. We alcoholics get isolated. We get insulated and isolated from God. We're afraid to go to church. We're afraid to sit down by ourselves to pray. We feel guilty. We feel uncomfortable in the presence of a Higher Power and so we do our best to hide from him. We may know intellectually that it is impossible, but we try it anyway. We knew it was impossible for us to drink safely, but we tried it anyway. It's a miserable state of alienation from the God of our understanding. We're hiding from him. We're hiding from ourselves. A common way of doing that is by lying about how much we're drinking. I would have a bottle and before I poured myself a drink, I'd take a swig out of the bottle. I'd think, "That's not a drink; that's just a little swig." You don't believe that? I don't think I did either, but I was telling myself that. I was hiding from the truth. When I would have one of those terrible hangovers and I would feel that I was dying, I'd crawl over to a mirror in my bathroom. I'd look in the mirror, and I'd pull my eyelid down and say, "By God, you're getting better. You're looking better than you looked a half an hour ago."

That was hiding from the truth about myself. I was afraid to take a look into my own interior. I was such a mess, so mixed up. I knew that as a priest, the way I was living was in complete contradiction with my profession, my priesthood. I was supposed to be a man who was available for other people. But I was hiding and I was no longer useful. I was hiding from myself, from you, and from God. I was pretending that I wasn't really drinking, that I wasn't as wobbly as I seemed to be. You know how that is. I was ducking around corners to avoid people. I was living in a community of fellow Jesuits. Some of them I went to high school with. They were close friends and I was ducking them. If I saw them coming down the corridor I would turn my head, and sidle into my room, close the door, and pull the shades. I was living in darkness and gloom. I was hiding.

The Fifth Step says, "We admitted to God, to ourselves and to another human being...." In the beginning, I tended to make too little of the first two beings, God and myself. I figured that happens automatically. The big thing that stuck out in my mind was admitting all this to another man. I was in hiding.

I think of wrongs in the Fifth Step in a wide sense, not just sins, not just things I might have done against my conscience or against the Commandments, but all the sick things that happened through alcoholic drinking, all the consequences of alcoholism—how it affected me, how it affected my companions and other people. It includes whatever I may have done against my conscience. Later on, with these papers in mind, I formally stood before God and said, "Lord, here I am. This is me. This is what has happened in my life." I had come out of hiding. From what has happened to me in AA, God has shown me that he has accepted that because things have gone well.

The hardest thing that I found was to admit it to myself. I knew in my mind that God knew all about me whether I admitted it or not. But I was hiding from me. I had my history down on paper, but there was something inside of me saying, "Well, maybe it didn't happen," or "If people only understood why I did this, they would understand that I wasn't this way." That is incredible rationalizing, hiding. This is where the Third Step comes in, to accept myself and my story, not just to admit it. It says to admit to God, to ourselves and to another human being the exact nature of our wrongs. To admit and to accept it, to stop trying to change it. To stop saying, for example, to the God of my understanding, "Lord, I wish I hadn't done that." That's a good thing to say. That's contrition, but thinking that that's going to change a fact is a mistake. The facts are there forever. What changes is the relationship between the individual and God. We're back in communication—back on a level of friendship—not distance, not darkness and hiding and running around corners, but meeting the God of our understanding in the daily events of life in and out of AA, in all the wonderful people we meet, and the miracles we come upon in AA. Then, I had to accept myself as a recovering alcoholic and insofar as I have been a sinner, like all human beings, to accept God's forgiveness—to reach out and take it. We accept the forgiveness he offers. After we've made our peace with him and expressed our sorrow and decided that with his grace we will do better—we don't keep saying, "I wonder if he really meant that? Did he really mean that? Do you think that God took a close enough look at me? How could he ever forgive me?"

We all think that the things we did were the worst things in the world. But very often they weren't. They were far from being the worst. I'm not saying things we did were not wrong.

Almighty God, as I understand him, will forgive anything, if I come and say to him, "Lord, here is my confession. Here is what I did. This is what happened to me. I want your forgiveness." To me, that was the most difficult part.

Then we admit to another human being. This one person is the representative of the human race. I began to restore my relationship with God, with myself, with you—my brothers and sisters, my fellow human beings, my fellow members. I began to restore my communication and my fellowship with you. This one man that I picked to be the recipient of my sad tale represents the human race. I think there should be one person—I don't think it should be scattered around. That way there is one other human being on the face of the earth who knows as much about me as I do, and he still loves me. He still accepts me.

I remember after I finished my Fourth Step, I pondered who I would ask to listen to my Fifth Step. At a meeting at Guest House, I heard about the distinction between Sacramental Confession which they have in the Catholic Church and the Fifth Step. I decided to ask a layman to listen to me. I wanted to make sure that I did not turn the Fifth Step into a Sacramental Confession—which I also need and I use. I asked Ripley—the director of Guest House—if he would listen to my Fifth Step, and he graciously acceded.

But I had to wait three weeks. During those three weeks— for a while anyway not for the whole three weeks—I nearly went mad. After he gave me the appointment, I went to my room and said, "Why in God's name did I do that? What if he sells my story to *Life Magazine*. After all he's a member of AA. He's a recovering alcoholic. He might get drunk and blab this. He might become a millionaire as I go down in everlasting disgrace with my story in *Life Magazine*." Now, that's alcoholic, isn't it? That's the ego. But you know I was tormented for a week or little more until it finally dawned on me, "Why don't you put this under the Third Step." So I did that. I put this coming disclosure, the Fifth Step, in the care of God. I did my best to believe, "God will be there as he is here today.

If anything goes wrong, the same God who cares for me will be there and he will give me his help. He might not remove every difficulty, but he will give me the strength I need to bear with him and to tolerate it without disaster." God gave me peace.

I went through the Fifth Step in three sessions, three hours a piece. I spent nine hours on it with this big sheaf of papers. I sat on one side of the table and Ripley was across from me. I got going, and a couple of times Rip popped in with stories of his own to encourage me and to make me feel better and by sharing that he, too, had some trouble. This was very uncharacteristic of me, but I was so eager to do this thing, I said, "Rip, will you just keep quiet!"

I can still see his face. It fell about a foot. I said, "I've got to get this thing done!" The poor guy sat there for three three-hour sessions, and I put him to sleep. This story of mine that was going to get him a million dollars from *Life Magazine* was enough to put him to sleep! But I plowed through the thing to be thorough. I was as thorough as I could be. I might have over done it. I don't know, but I've never looked back on that and wished that I hadn't been so thorough.

One reason I was afraid to start the Fifth Step with Rip was that I admired him so much. He really saved my life. He was a wonderful man. I wanted to have his friendship, at least his good disposition. I was afraid that after he heard me his attitude towards me would change. I knew he would be polite. He was a gentleman. But I was afraid that my Fifth Step would mark the end of a beautiful friendship. I was really afraid of that. But I put it under the Third Step. And do you know what happened? We became better friends. We became closer friends. I was out there for a long time and later on he shared things with me, and I was able to be a help to him in some ways. I could hardly believe it.

This is what I said in the beginning about the Fourth and the Fifth Steps—they have just the opposite effect to what we feel. I noticed that after I did my Fifth Step, I was able to stay by myself and to sit in my room peacefully. I didn't have to get up and do something or get out. I was beginning to be able to put up with myself. Before the Fifth Step, I hated myself. I was so disappointed in my performance as a priest. Miraculously that disappeared. I was able to sit down quietly and think, or pray, or meditate. I also had a deeper sense of belonging.

I was in the program seven months before I spoke at an open meeting. Most of the meetings I went to in Michigan were step discussions meetings. But I gave my first AA talk at a meeting in Detroit. I had to fight through it, of course. I stood up and said, "I'm an alcoholic. I'm an alcoholic priest." And after that talk, I felt I really belonged.

The Fifth Step deepened that sense of belonging. It also gave me the feeling of satisfaction. After I left that third session with Ripley—I banged my hand and I said, "I did it." There was a feeling of having done something quite difficult and done it to the best of my ability. It lifted me up.

Dr. Walter G., an old-timer in AA who has been dead many years now, used to come to our place and talk about the disease of alcoholism. I learned an awful lot from him. Every now and then he would give a real wonderful AA talk. He made this suggestion to those doing the Fifth Step, he said, "After you've done the Fifth Step, take the papers, and make a little ritual out of them, and burn them. Put them in the incinerator and burn them. That symbolizes the end of that life and the beginning of a new life." I did that. Naturally, being an alcoholic, a few times later on, I said I wish I had those papers back. But I think it was a good suggestion.

After I finished the Fifth Step, Ripley said to me, "Now, go downtown and get yourself a whole new outfit from the skin out." I did that, too—a new way of life.

I still go to Fifth Step meetings and they help me. I don't learn much of anything that's new. What happens to me is that the things I already know get deeper. I know them better. This is very important. Sometimes I see the connection between things. That reveals me to myself a little better.

I've listened to many Fifth Steps since I've been in the program. I did it for years. I had to discontinue that a few years ago. I had some kind of affliction that was stopping blood and oxygen from getting to my brain. People would be talking to me and, against my will, I would nod off. I think I hurt some people. They must have thought that I wasn't interested. I was fighting to hold my head up. It wasn't the lack of sleep, it was whatever this affliction was. I've had it somewhat corrected since. But I decided I better stop listening to Fifth Steps and doing this because I thought I was hurting more people than I was helping. Besides it had gotten to be a terrible burden for me.

For what it's worth, I'll tell you one more thing I have experienced with the Fifth Step. I'm not absolutely certain that this is the best thing to do, but I have met people in AA who would get a bit of their Fourth Step done and then get bogged down. They just couldn't seem to go any further. I suggested to a few of these people, that they share what they had written so far with me or with whoever they had asked to listen to the step. It worked. They got what they had written off their mind. It freed them to move on and do some more. On a number of occasions, we did it in stages. It might have taken three or four or five sessions before they got through the whole thing.

We used to have a Canadian doctor, Gordon Bell, who worked in the field of addiction. He had a clinic in a suburb of Toronto. While I was at Guest House, he visited us on three different occasions. He was a blackboard lecturer who would lecture all day. We would stop every couple of hours and have a cup of coffee. I still remember that man and what he taught me.

Here is one of the stories that he told us that might fit into what we are thinking about tonight: In his clinic in Willowdale, he had sessions for alcohol and for heavy drugs, for tranquilizers, smoking, and food. He talked about a woman who came to visit him. After she had her first child she got addicted to food. Over-eating is a carbon copy of alcoholism. She began to eat and to do the same type of things that we alcoholics do. She would have a big meal before her husband got home from work, then she would clean up the table and sit down with him and eat another meal as though she hadn't eaten. She began to put on a lot of weight. She went to a doctor and he put her on pills, amphetamines. Instead of being helped with the food addiction, she now had two addictions—one to food, the other to pills.

Eventually, she came to his clinic and she opened her purse and poured out hundreds of these pills on his desk. Then she made a statement that is a classic description of addiction. She said, "I love them because they're able to do for me what people can't do."

The alcoholic needs to be restored to the human race.

–Admitted to God, to myself, and another human being exactly who I am.

We need people. Look at the gift we have in Alcoholics Anonymous. Think of all the hundreds, maybe thousands of people that Old Tony met in his lifetime in AA. Think of all the people that man touched. And think of all the people you and I share with—even people whose names we don't know—but we know them as fellow addicts, alcoholics, drug addicts. We can share with them. We can open up and we can say things to one another. We don't have to draw a map. We know each other. We know how the thing works and what a blessing it is that we have each other, that we have the fellowship. I think of the fellowship as a fellowship and a program. It's a fellowship which is using this program. That's AA. I need the program, not just a part of it, and I need you. I suppose it's a commonplace thing, that I become me by sharing with you. I can't do it alone. I can't remain in hiding from God, myself, and my neighbor and hope to grow. It is by coming out of isolation through this Fifth Step and sharing with God, with myself, and with another human being, that I come out into the daylight. I need you. It can be a real encounter between real people who are not lying to themselves or to God or to others—people who are seriously and truthfully facing the problem, and honestly, with God's help, doing something about it. If there are any people here who are still struggling with these inventory steps, I think the best thing that we other alcoholics can do is to encourage you to give it a try. It has worked for so many people. If you have the thought, "It won't work for me," do your best to set that aside and believe in the experience of AA. The first couple of hundred successful alcoholics in whose name Bill W. penned The Big Book said that they tried to find an easier way and it didn't work. They found that we had to do this and they begged us to be thorough. If you're facing this thing and you're afraid of it, we are afraid, too. But if we could face it and plow through it and experience the wonderful effects of those steps, you can, too.

Thank you very much, all of you.

# Step Six

*"Became entirely ready to have God remove all our defects of character."*

This was listed on the program monitor as a Twelve Step Meeting, but it's not really a meeting. I was asked by a couple of friends to talk about the Twelve Steps, one at a time. The original idea was to do it in a private home with a few people just to give me somebody to talk to or talk at. They decided to move up here and it's grown. I think one of the reasons for this is that a lot of us AA members are really interested in the steps of recovery. That's why I'm interested. I'm glad you are here. Thank you for coming.

So far we have talked about the first five steps. It's commonly agreed that the first three steps are the foundation of the program. They deal immediately with the different aspects of our disease of alcoholism—our addiction. The physical is stressed in the First Step; the mental and the emotional are stressed in the Second Step; and what we call the spiritual or the disorder in the will is stressed in the Third Step. Self-centered, self-will is carefully described in The Big

Book in the Fifth Chapter. When we get the first three steps working together in our lives—even though they are not working perfectly—we find out what is meant by sobriety. I knew from experience what is meant by being dry. By getting these three steps together, working together, then I began to experience sobriety. That is not only freedom from alcohol, but it is the beginning of freedom from alcoholic thinking, sick, destructive emotions, and self-centered self-will.

I got out of the driver's seat and I began to rely on a power greater than myself. I turned everything over to his loving care. This took some months in the program, but when it came about in my life, I found out how different sobriety is from mere dryness. The members of AA, who stood behind The Big Book, learned from their experience that if they wanted to maintain sobriety and have it as a permanent day by day reality in their lives, they needed to change. They found that if their personalities remained as they were before they stopped drinking, there was a real danger of returning to alcohol. This was a knowledge that came out of their experience. It didn't come out of a scientific book—it came out of the experience of the first successful members of AA.

They tell us in The Big Book that they tried to find an easier way and it didn't work. In order to begin this change in ourselves, we have to find out who we are—what our strong points are and what are our weaknesses. We accomplish that in the Fourth Step. That step speaks of a searching and fearless investigation of ourselves. Both those words are well chosen. I needed to overcome the fear of looking more closely at myself in order to do the step. "Searching"—I was lazy. I didn't like the thought of the work that would be involved in combing through my life and getting enough words on paper so that later on I'd have a clear understanding of the way it was with me. These papers also help us to do the Fifth Step in which we came out of hiding and "admitted to God, to ourselves, and to another human being the exact nature of our wrongs." Those are the only three relationships that are possible for us human beings.

We were hiding. I was hiding from God, although I knew that it was futile. I was certainly hiding from myself. I didn't want to look carefully at myself. And I sure as heck was hiding from you, and my associates, my neighbors. I didn't want anybody to look inside me and get a glimpse of what had been going on there. The Fifth Step, which we talked about last week, is standing before God and saying, "Here Lord, here is my story." Then calling myself to look and saying, "Look. Fred, look. That's you. That's what you did. That's what happened to you. That's not somebody else. That's you." I think the main reason why I reached a point where I could do that without disaster was that I had the Third Step working in my life sufficiently to enable me to accept my real self and my real history. Then sharing this with another human being. Not with a number of them, but with one human being who to me would represent the human race. By opening up myself completely to the best of my ability to this other person, I came out of hiding.

I soon began to experience some of the good effects of the Fourth and Fifth Steps. I stopped running away from myself. I became able to sit down by myself and think or pray or read quietly. That was a very noticeable benefit for me. Another benefit, maybe even more important than that, was that I began to feel that I belonged. I belonged to AA, and I belonged to the human race. Until then, I felt that I was looking at life through a plate glass window. I was an outsider. After I did the Fifth Step that feeling was gone. I could see myself more realistically as just another human being with this disease.

In The Twelve and Twelve, it says that after a person has done the Fifth Step he should take a little rest. Years ago I said that to a friend of mine who made his Fifth Step to me. I gave him that little bit of advice right out of The Book. He told me later that he rested for six years. That's not the idea. That's taking a chance.

The Sixth Step is where we become entirely ready to have God remove all these defects. What defects? The defects that showed up in the Fourth and Fifth Steps. In my opinion, that includes defects that I'm not aware of. Even though I did my best with the inventory, I feel that I must have other short-comings or defects. Incidentally, Bill Wilson said that by those two words—defects and shortcomings—he meant the same thing. He just wanted to vary the language.

I'm convinced that one of the hardest things in the world is for us to know ourselves thoroughly. In the Sixth Step, I include the defects that I knew about, the ones shared with my sponsor in the Fifth Step. Some of the things that showed up in my inventory were things that I did or thought when I was in command of myself. I wasn't drunk twenty-four hours a day. The inventory deals with my whole life. I didn't start drinking until I was almost twenty-five years old, but I had to examine the years I wasn't drinking, too. Some of the things that show up in the inventory have to do with my conscience—things that I did knowingly and willing against my conscience and against God. I'm not talking necessarily about big crimes. But the main defects that show up are traits of character. They are emotional upsets, emotional tendencies or what are called the seven capital sins. They are tendencies in us human beings. They are part of the human condition. For example, we have a tendency towards pride. It's a human thing. There are other impulses in me that are part of humanity. A defect can be something excessive. For example, think of a virtue like courage. The defect can be on either side of it. It may be I don't have enough courage. Perhaps, I'm a person who is often been afraid to step out and tackle a new job or meet different people. I'm timid. I'm lacking in courage. On the other side, if I have an excess of courage I could be rash. I step in where angels fear to tread. I try to clear out the barroom and I get murdered. But that doesn't stop my rashness. I try it again. I've got courage to burn. It isn't courage, it's rashness. It's a kind of insanity. Am I fearful, anxious, timid? These are not sins. We don't know how they originate in us. We aren't that way on purpose. We don't choose to feel anxious. We just feel that way. That's a defect.

Doing the Sixth Step is like starting the program all over again. But now we are not dealing with alcohol or drugs, we are dealing with our defects. We're dealing with these traits that need to be changed. These are things that could make it easier for us to pick up drink.

There can be a misconception about the Sixth Step. Some people think that it is saying that now that we are sober and are doing the first three steps and we've done our inventory and the Fifth Step—it's time to roll up our sleeves and become saints. That turns some people off. I'm not against becoming a saint. I'm all for it. But that's not what the Sixth Step is about. The Sixth Step is about my disease. If these defects don't help to lead me back to the first drink, they at least stop my recovery. They prevent me from fully recovering. They leave me sick to a certain degree. If I'm in the program and I'm still afraid of people, I'm afraid to talk to someone or to ask someone for a favor—to that extent I remain less than par. I have not grown up emotionally.

This step is to free us of any thing in us that stops us from growing up. To me, this step starts the program of recovery from alcoholism. It will also help us to become better persons. But what we are focusing on here is, how can we grow up? How can we change? How can we use this step to be healthier people? This isn't a sudden change from recovery to religion. It's still recovery. It will help me also in my practice of religion. But my reason for doing this step is to advance in my recovery from this total personality disorder. The Sixth Step is like the First Step. It's starting the program again, but this time on my personality disorders or defects. The words "Were entirely ready to have God remove all these defects all these shortcomings" implies a couple of things. First that sentence implies that I am willing—that I have honesty and open-mindedness. It also implies that I admit I can't do it myself. What is it that I can't do? I can't reach inside of myself and take this whole bundle of defects and throw it over my shoulder and get rid of them once and for all. I don't have that power. I'm just as powerless in that area as I am over alcohol, and I admit that. The meaning of the Sixth Step to me is that I admit that I am powerless over these defects. I also admit that they might make my life less comfortable. Experience shows that I'm in danger of turning back to alcohol if I don't change. And if I do that it may be curtains for me. So the Sixth Step implies my admission that I have these defects that make my life unmanageable to a degree and that I'm powerless over them here and now. I stress here and now. Suppose I worked on one of them. Let's say I had a tendency to fly off the handle. If I were to work on that defect day after day—and I asked God's help each day and I tried to resist that tendency and sought help from other members, I think after a period of time, I could change that. What I can't do is change it here and now. And I certainly can't change the whole bundle of defects here and now.

"Were entirely ready." Look at those frightening words—we were ready. "I don't have any reservations. There is nothing holding me back. I am entirely ready to have you, God, my Higher Power, remove all of these defects." In my opinion, that's looking at the step in its literal meaning.

When we go to meetings on the Sixth Step, sometimes we talk about one defect that's been bugging us. It's entering into our life more frequently and causing us difficulty. We can use the principle involved in this step and become entirely ready to have God remove that defect. I'm not saying this isn't right. But the step literally is talking about all our defects. It says, "Were entirely ready to have God remove all." I think that's why, when The Twelve and Twelve introduces the Sixth Step, it says, "Here is the step that separates the men from the boys."

It also says that this step states an ideal objective. We are not aiming now at some lesser objective. We are aiming at the best. If we do that are we likely to achieve that end? Are we likely to reach a point where all of our defects have been removed from us? Common experience says that's not likely. The Book points out that even a great man like St. Paul didn't have that happen to him. It is a part of our humanity to be

threatened by these defects. The progress we can make is perhaps to let God remove some of them, and to have God
remove the frequency of which we slip into them and slide
back. If we do that we grow. It's painful. "Pain is the touchstone of growth" as we hear so often. For me to be changed by
God, by the same caring Power that gave us this program, can
be painful.

We often say that this is a God-given program. We believe
that. It appeared in this world a little over a half a century ago.
Why didn't something like it appear before? It is a mystery
why God waited so long, but he gave it to us. We all got here
by different routes, but he invited each one of us to come into
this program. "But for the grace of God." The first grace that
was given to us was an introduction to AA—the grace of
becoming willing to reach out for help. Because of that we
came to AA. God sustained us and helped us, and we kept
coming. It wasn't easy, but we kept coming. Finally, we came
to this stage, Step Six, where we are aiming at the best. I
believe the main reason for that is that if we aim high and we
keep aiming high, we are going to achieve something, but if
we aim low, at a more limited objective, the arrow is liable not
to reach the target. It's something like the statement that we
repeat so often—halfway measures avail us nothing.

The Sixth Step states an objective that's certainly not
halfway. It's all the way—"were entirely ready." It doesn't say
that we were entirely ready to have God help us to wrestle with
our defects and to throw them out. We've already admitted
powerlessness over them. It states the truth precisely—"Were
entirely ready to have God remove all of these defects"—just
as in the First Step we became entirely ready to have God keep
us away from the first drink and/or the first drug. There is a
sentence in The Big Book that is often quoted that says that at
certain times the only thing that stands between the addict
and the first drink or the first drug is God—a Higher Power.
This underlines the notion of powerlessness over a particular
thing. Being entirely ready to have God remove all of these
defects is an attitude that is strange to us. That may be

because of the culture we were brought up in. We hear so often that you can do anything you want, just roll up your sleeves and get in there and fight and you can accomplish it. There is some truth in that, but it is not entirely true. There are some things we can't accomplish no matter how many muscles we have and no matter how smart we are.

One thing I can't accomplish is that I cannot safely drink alcohol. Another thing I can't accomplish is I cannot continue to stay away from the first drink by my own thinking, no matter how many meetings I've gone to, how many books I've read, or how many people I've seen die from alcoholism. I have this disease. The disease is a three-fold powerlessness. Sure I can stay away from the first drink by my thinking sometimes, maybe for a fairly long time, but I can't continue to do it.

So there is powerlessness over these defects. But the same God who protects me a day at a time from alcohol can change me. He protects me from the first drink or the first drug, and protects me a day at a time from alcoholic or addictive thinking and the subtle insanity that goes before the first drink or drug. If I get out of the drivers seat and let that same God who cares for me take over, he can change me. It isn't likely that he is going to erase all these defects in one fell swoop. It isn't that he can't do it, but it doesn't look as though he works that way. Many who have been in the program for a while know how the use of this step, even though we fall short of the ideal objective, really brings about a gradual change in the way we live. We grow and we deal with life in a much more mature way.

I have often pondered the phrase, "Were entirely ready" and asked myself how we do that.

One way, a negative way, is to consider what might happen to me if I don't change, if I don't use this step. I didn't say what will certainly happen to me, but what might happen to me. It at least will be this: I won't make much progress. I won't grow much beyond where I am. I may never drink again, but I may not gain from the program all that it has to offer. A positive way is to think about what will happen to me if I do it. How good life could be if, for example, I could be delivered from my tendency to procrastinate or other defects. There are many examples of defects. Suppose I could be less touchy or I could get rid of perfectionism. Wouldn't it be wonderful if I was less subject to those defects. So that's the second way to become ready.

A third way, which may be the best way of all, is to pray to become entirely ready—to ask God to make us more and more willing to have him remove all of these defects.

It can be frightening. What would happen if God removed my procrastination right away? What would I do with myself?

This image occurred to me while wondering what happens when God removes our defects. When I was a boy we had a stereoptic machine. It was like a magic lantern with a candle in it. You hung up a sheet on a wall and you got a post card or a picture and you put it in the machine and it projected the picture on the sheet. It was wonderful entertainment long before the Second World War. But the point is: how did you remove the picture that was in there? You removed it by putting another picture in. It was a process. You put the second picture in gently from one end and the first picture would slide over and the second one slid in. You don't go from black to white. God gives us the new virtue or the new trait bit by bit. By giving us a little bit of it, out goes a little bit of the old bad trait. It's a gradual thing. Sometimes we don't notice that it's happening, that we're changing. Then there comes a time later when we may realize that we are different. It's very encouraging, very satisfying. We can say with conviction, "The program really works. It really works."

I'll conclude with this—something that's been very important to me. One of the things that made it difficult in the beginning to turn away from alcohol was fear. "What will life be without alcohol?" Part of that was the mythology that, "If I can't drink, at least occasionally, how can I be happy? How can I be satisfied? If I can't drink say on Thanksgiving and Christmas and at the big football game, how can I be a happy person?" Being addicted at this time and so totally dependent on alcohol, that seemed like an impossibility not to have it and to be happy.

"Under the lash of alcoholism," as it says, we come into the program and we follow suggestions and after a while we are free of alcohol and we are reasonably happy. That's the miracle of AA—not just that we stop drinking or drugging but that we become happy. We find out that the idea that you cannot be happy without alcohol and/or drugs is a lie. It's a damn lie. That lie had us in its grips for many years before the program.

Now, we might say, "How could I live without this defect or that defect? I'll admit it's a second hand way of dealing with life, but I've been doing it all my life and I'm very comfortable with it. It's familiar to me. How am I going to get along in life if that's taken away from me?" It's a big, big block, but I think that we should know what happened to us through the First Step and our practice of it—we found out that we could be happy without alcohol. If we had enough faith and enough willingness, we could find out that we can be happy without that defect. It is all dependence on a Higher Power. There are so many things that we can't do by ourselves that God will do for us if we turn to him. I know sometimes when I make my own prayers and I'm praying for some growth or some virtue, I'm afraid that it is going to ask too much of me, spiritually. But with the help of this program and other help, I ask for it anyway. That's an act of courage. I rely on God not only to give it to me, but to make me ready to receive it. It's a total dependence on God.

This is all I have to say about the Sixth Step tonight. I'm very appreciative towards you for your kind attention.

Thank you.

# Step Seven

*"Humbly asked him to remove all of our shortcomings."*

Greetings everybody. I'm sorry about last week. I forgot to warn you beforehand that there would be no meeting. It was what they call Spring Break. They let the students loose for a week. Any time the students go home, this building isn't open at night, unless they have some real big wingding going on here. I forgot to warn you about that. But I'll warn you about this one—we won't have a meeting here on Good Friday, that's April the 14th. On the other Fridays, we have just enough Fridays left, counting tonight, God willing, to finish the Twelve Steps. So that will bring us up to the 5th of May. That will be the last meeting like this. I'll remind you again, if I remember. It must be very disappointing to come here and find the doors closed.

When I was fifty-one and had a little over a year in the program, I went to a three day convention in New York for members of the clergy who are alcoholics. This was the second such convention that I had attended. My first was at Notre Dame while I was still out at Guest House. We drove about five hours to get there. Austin Ripley, the director of Guest House, and about fifteen of us priests went. Rip told us that we probably would not learn an awful lot, but he said the experience would be valuable because of the people we would meet, the members of AA and other people who are interested in the problem. What I remember most about that convention was the closing talk. It was given by the Catholic Bishop of the diocese there. He was an impromptu speaker, filling in for the final speaker who didn't show up. His talk was a simple one. The gist of it was that it was about time the laity in the Catholic Church grew up about this subject of alcoholism. But he asked how could the laity grow up if the priests don't? He was stressing the teaching, so familiar to us, that alcoholism in itself is not a moral problem. It can have moral consequences, but in itself it is a complicated illness that has to be treated in the right way. That talk has remained in my memory.

I also remember some of the people I met there, in particular a doctor who had moved from New York to Michigan and carried on his practice there. He told me the reason he moved was that he got sick and tired of living in the asphalt jungle and wanted to see some trees. Isn't it wonderful to remember that? It doesn't help you at all, but it has helped me over the years. I often think of him and say, "Gee, what a man."

I heard Bill Wilson talk for the first, last and only time at the conference in New York. I can still see him. As you know he was a tall man. He spoke very deliberately, slowly, very thoughtfully, and I believe he was a humble man. He said the steps of the program were first expressed in six steps, but after a while it was decided to take the same material and divide it into parts, not changing anything, but just stating it in individual parts. He said that was to make it so clear that not even an alcoholic could miss them. We still manage to miss them. But that stuck in my memory, too.

In the first AA groups that I belonged to there were step discussion meetings. We didn't use The Twelve and Twelve at the meeting. We had a little yellow pamphlet that would give a page or a page and a half of suggestions about each step, just about enough to prime the pump and give you a little material to start a discussion. This booklet treated the Sixth and the Seventh Step together as it did the Eighth and the Ninth. But in The Twelve and Twelve, they are treated singly. In view of what Bill W. said, I'm taking Six and Seven one at a time. I talked about the Sixth Step. Tonight, I'll try to share with you whatever it is that I've learned about the Seventh Step.

Most of us alcoholics are very impatient. That is part of our makeup. We want to get the job done and get it out of the way so we can relax for the next forty years. As a result we are liable to skip over something. For example, in the Sixth Step it says, "Were entirely ready." We could think that wasn't of great importance because it's not doing something with our muscles. It's something that we do with our minds and with our will and with our hearts. But that is the action in the Sixth Step. It's spiritual in the sense that it's inside of us. It's performed by the spiritual part of our humanity. That includes our thinking power, our willing power, our hearts, our desires and our intentions. All of that goes on inside of us. That's where we're sick. When we first come to the program, we don't want to admit that we have a problem with alcohol and that we are alcoholics. We lie to ourselves. We hide. We are certainly not entirely ready to have God remove the first drink just for the day, not right away. There are exceptions to this. But for many of us, it's a process, an interior spiritual action of becoming entirely ready.

We know the means that we used in the past to become ready to ask God to keep us away from the first drink. That took a long time for many of us. It was intense action of reading and listening to other people and going to meetings, but mainly of taking our own inventory. It's painful, hard work. It's spiritual, not necessarily religious, but spiritual. By spiritual I mean something inside of me that's very real but it's different from my body. It's what makes me keep going—what directs me and guides me.

We talked about "Were entirely ready to have God remove all these defects" the last time. I'm referring back to it to underline that "Were entirely ready" means something that I'm still laboring at. It's an interior spiritual action. I still ask myself at times if I'm "entirely ready to have God remove all the defects in me"—the ones I saw in the Fifth Step and the ones I don't know about. When I'm honest with myself as I try to be, I don't think that I am entirely ready.

If there was ever a daily step, it's the Sixth and Seventh Steps. It's true of all the steps, of course, but it's especially true of these.

Now it doesn't say we became entirely ready to roll up our sleeves and do the job ourselves. We become entirely ready to have God do it. Sometimes, we say, "I'm working on this." What am I working on? It's easy to think that we will make greater efforts to overcome these defects. That's good. I'm not decrying that. But that's not what the step says. The step says, "Were entirely ready to have God remove all these defects." It's like the First Step, where we became entirely ready to have God keep us away from the first drink.

Of course we contribute to this by going to meetings and talking with recovering alcoholics, reading The Big Book, following the suggestions, saying the Serenity Prayer, and trying to live the slogans. Conversely, we will stay out of barrooms. We frequent a lounge to play cards or go into barrooms to buy cigarettes. We stay away from that. That's an external action that we can do. The only thing we can't do by ourselves is have power over alcohol. So how can we become entirely ready to have God remove these defects? The question is answered in the Seventh Step. We humbly ask him to remove all these shortcomings.

There used to be discussions that would arise at meetings, "Why did he say defects in the Sixth Step and shortcomings in the Seventh? Is he talking about different things or the same things?" It was a question that was posed to Bill himself who penned the steps. He gave the answer in an old *Grapevine* that I found years ago. I can't remember the date of the issue, but I remember his answer. He said he meant the same thing. He was just trying to vary the expression a little bit. So the shortcomings mentioned in the Seventh Step are the same as the defects mentioned in the Sixth.

The step says that after I become entirely ready—or I'm getting close to it—then I humbly ask God to remove these shortcomings. We don't get frantic and say, "Let me at them. I'll clean these out." That's booze fighting with our own defects and it doesn't work anymore than it would work with booze itself. The phrase, "Humbly asked him to remove" is alien to us. We're not used to thinking that way. Not only as self-willed alcoholics but in our culture. We've been brought up to believe in rugged individualism. We are told that if we make our minds up, we can do whatever we want. That doesn't work here. We are dealing with a deadly addiction—a personality disorder— that is a killer. It's insidious, baffling, cunning, destructive. We are told in The Book, and we know from our experience, that no earthly power can remove the obsession from us. This step is the same thing. "We humbly ask him to remove all these shortcomings."

We think of these defects as things that can get us back to alcohol. The main intention here is not being a good Christian. I hope that happens. But I'm doing the step because I don't want to maintain within me some attitude in the mind or the will that will get me back to alcohol. If I go back to alcohol I'm a goner.

By the time I had my last drink, I wanted to die. What would it be for me if, God forbid, I should be moved by something in me like pride to be crazy enough to pick up a drink? I think that's what is important here. We want to get rid of whatever it is in our makeup that could lead us back to a drink. They may be things that bother our conscience, things that we did on purpose, things that disturb us and make us feel uneasy in the presence of God. We never know which one of them can come up and trigger off that insane thinking that goes before the first drink. I'm not recommending living in fear. I don't live in fear. I'm trying to appreciate the importance of this step. I'm already on the way towards being entirely ready to have God remove these things. Now I humbly ask him. The action is the asking. In order to express the idea you don't even need the word "humbly." If I ask you for something, I've got to at least have enough humility to know my place—to ask and not to demand. Not having humility would be like walking up to a fellow and saying, "Look, give me a match for my cigarette or I'll knock your head off. Don't you know who I am?" The step says that the difference between a simple request and a demand is obvious.

So the asking. We grow in our conception of the Higher Power, of the God of our understanding, and see what happens to ourselves and to others in the program. Isn't it wonderful when you're around for a while to see a newcomer come in. At the first meeting, sometimes you can hardly recognize him or her as an ordinary human being. They're so beaten. Sometimes, especially with some men, they're physically beaten. They've been in a fight where they were almost slaughtered. Maybe that's what brought them to their senses. They come to the meeting and they can't hold a cup of coffee. You see them week after week, and after a reasonable time they begin to appear as human beings. You can see recovery happening in them. As we often hear in AA, the only one we are asking is God. We can hardly avoid the thought, "Isn't it wonderful. Look at how good God is. Look at how good God is being to that man or that woman." After a while we begin to think, "How good he is to me."

We don't have to get him in a headlock. We don't have to throttle him and demand that he give us this recovery. We ask him. And the asking by itself is humbling. By the very act and the manner of asking, I recognize that he is superior to me, that I am needy. I need what only he can give me. That's enough humility.

Now, even when I'm asking God in that way, I may still have an awful lot of pride in me. I might still be unwilling or reluctant to ask you to do me a favor. I may still have this pride in me that's telling me I should be able to take care of myself and to do everything that I need for me. I'm far from being an example of real, deep humility, but I have enough humility to ask God. I say this because I found out for myself that if I get too interested in whether I'm humble or not, I'm overlooking the action in the step which is to ask God to remove all these shortcomings.

Both the Sixth and the Seventh Steps as they are written are universal. "Were entirely ready to have God remove all these defects. Humbly asked him to remove all these short-comings." As it tells us in The Book, we're aiming at a very high goal in asking this. Especially when we think of our Fourth and Fifth Steps, and we have some better appreciation of how weak we are—how many defects we have. We have a better appreciation of how sensitive or fearful or angry or resentful or self-pitying we are. There is the famous sentence in The Big Book that says that self-centered fear is the chief activator of our defects. What a very revealing and important sentence that is. Self-centered fear is fear that I'm not going to get something that I think I have to have in order to be happy and successful. For example, I may want to get a very important job in the company so that everybody who knows me will think I'm important. So, perhaps, I have a conviction that if I don't make it big, I'm a nobody. But I have another conviction that's contradictory. I'm low on self-esteem. I'm afraid that I can never accomplish what I want. There is confusion of these emotions. Self-centered fear—fear that I'm not going to get something that I'm convinced I have to have in order to be happy, or fear that I'm going to lose something that is very precious to me now. I may fear losing some possession or my house or my car or my money or my health or my eyesight. You can run through a whole catalog of things to fear losing.

At Guest House, Ripley would often state his own con-viction that fear is the basic emotion in an alcoholic. That may not be universally true but it's true in some of us, maybe in many of us. It's true of me.

These defects of character are second-rate ways of dealing with reality. When I first came to the program and I looked ahead at Steps Six and Seven, I said to myself, "Oh that will be easy when I come to it." But when I did come to them, I found out that they are not so easy. There are some defects, some second-rate ways of facing reality, that I have, that are so familiar to me and that I rely on so much, that I'm afraid to let go of them.

At a meeting at Austin Street I heard a speaker who was a golfer and he illustrated his meaning by talking about golf. He gave the example of man who keeps hitting a slice, a banana ball, off the tee. The ball goes out and curves to the right. It's no good. It doesn't go very far. So somebody tells him to move his right hand a quarter inch to the left. He does that but it's quite uncomfortable for him. He swings and he hits the ball out straight. He goes along pretty well for awhile but now comes the crunch where he has to hit a long ball to stay in the game. What does he do? He falls back into his familiar way of holding the club. What happens? He hits another slice.

That's a pretty good illustration that left to myself, I can avoid some of these defects for awhile. But when the going gets tough or when I get tired, I go back to the old way of doing it. I'm back with some second rate way of dealing with reality.

We are taught in the program that in order to maintain our sobriety happily and to have a better guarantee of continued sobriety, we have to change. Or we have to be changed—it might be better to put it that way. We have to be willing to let God change us. If we can maintain the attitude of humbly asking God today to remove our shortcomings, we are less likely to fall into the old habitual ways of doing things. Those old ways are not mature. They're emotionally immature. But I love them because I'm so used to them. It's a way that I have lived for many years without realizing it.

This is a change that is painful. We believe in the program that pain is the touchstone of progress. For us to use these steps day by day and to change or let God change us, at times is extremely painful.

This is an example we hear many times from speakers in AA. A fellow who runs into somebody else who contradicts or even insults him. His old automatic manner would be to retaliate. But now with the growing wisdom of AA and his reliance on a Higher Power, he reaches a point of much greater maturity. He doesn't react in an emotionally childish way. That doesn't mean he will allow some other man to walk all over him. The program doesn't call for that. But now his reaction is different. The old way had a lot of emotional defects in it, hurt pride and vanity, the desire to get even and to put the other fellow in his place. That's the way it was back in grammar school days. When I was a kid, if some new kid showed up in the neighborhood, we would all wonder if we could lick him. That's very appropriate for a child. But when you're forty-five years old and somebody says I want you to meet Mr. Harrison, and while your shaking hands with him, you're saying, "I wonder if I could beat this guy up…"

The defects that are mentioned as killers are resentment and self-pity. There are many others, of course, but AA experience shows that resentment and self-pity are the number one and number two killers. The word "resentment" means to experience a thing over and over. Ten years ago somebody called me a bad name and I reacted with anger. Ever since, when I remember that, I relive it in my memory and my imagination. I go through the same thing over and over. And every time I do, another layer of hurt feelings and sickness builds up in my memory and in my soul.

The Big Book says that the reason resentment is the number one killer is that it cuts off the light of the spirit. When we are beginning to get sober and we are relying on God, or a Higher Power, we have a sort of light—a little bit of uplift in the heart. There is a little bit of joy and a little touch of happiness. We know that we're on the right road

and that AA will work. Then along comes something negative. We have a quarrel with somebody. Somebody insults us
or belittles us. If we react with resentment and we don't solve
it right away, in a grown up manner, but instead, we relive it,
it closes off that light. It's most difficult for an alcoholic to
stay sober when anything like joy or satisfaction or happiness
is cut out of the picture. Then existence is just a dark miserable experience. It means doing without something inside of
us that we want very much. There doesn't seem to be much
reward for existing. That is why resentment is such a killer.

Resentment and self-pity are like heads and tails on a dime.
If we have one, we have the other. In one case the person may
be more conscious of the resentment than the self-pity.
Another person may be more conscious of the self-pity than of
the resentment.

In the beginning I couldn't find out who I was angry
with. I thought that I didn't have any resentments, that I was
not blaming anybody—my family, my friends, or my religious order. But after a while, I became aware of the fact,
through my Fifth Step, that I was angry with God. That to
me was so horrible I couldn't put it into words. I couldn't
allow it to come into my consciousness. But I discovered by
his goodness and the help of this program that I was resentful
with God. I think that my resentment went something like
this, "God, you invited me into this religious life. You called
me to the priesthood. I went through all these years of study
and preparation, and then when I got into this trouble and I
pleaded with you to help me, you didn't help me." Of course,
I never allowed that to come to the forefront of my consciousness, but I believe it was there. Then through the help
of the program, I discovered that he had heard me and he
had answered me in a most magnificent, generous way, by
leading me into this program. That solved that resentment
for me.

I was more conscious of the self-pity. Of course when I
was indulging in it, I was still an active alcoholic. I wasn't
aware of what I was doing or how childish it was. I could lie

in bed for hours putting a movie on in my own head. "What a wonderful fellow I am, what a benefactor to the human race, and nobody even looks at me." I used to feel sorry because people couldn't look into me and see how much I was suffering. That's self-centeredness. Resentment and self-pity are killers. Once we become aware of the danger, we see how immature they are. Why should I be spending time, ten or twenty years later, rehearsing some injury that happened twenty years ago? What kind of a jackass am I to waste my time doing that when I could be doing something profitable or something pleasant? It's the same with self-pity.

*over & over about growing up*

It all adds up to emotional immaturity. We find that out through this program. My emotional growth was nowhere near my chronological age. It has nothing to do with whether you know your job or not. I knew what I had studied. Inside, emotionally, I was the same kind of a person I was when I was about nine years old. What a shock that is when we realize it. But for me, it turned into a great motivation. I used to say to myself, "I'm willing to do anything that will help me grow up so I can become a man and be a priest and I can reach a certain growth of manhood before I die." That has been one of the powerful motivations for me in going to meetings and trying to live this program.

Years ago a friend of mine in AA who was a member of Austin Street used to introduce his talks by giving his name and saying that he was an alcoholic and that he came to AA because he wanted to become a man. That touched me very much because that was what I wanted, too—to grow up.

This marvelous program is so simple that I think you can write the whole thing in a hundred and twenty eight words or something like that. But what a God given method of therapy it is if we use it. We put all the steps to work day by day, and continue in the Sixth and Seventh Steps to ask God to come into our lives. We are ready and we ask him to do for us what we can't do for ourselves.

"We will do what we can. We'll cooperate. We'll go to meetings. We'll do our best to cooperate with the change, but you, Lord, you my Higher Power, you are the one and the only one who can bring this about in me. So I am now humbly asking you to remove all of these shortcomings."

Thank you.

# Step Eight

*"Made a list of all persons we had harmed, and became willing to make amends to them all."*

Greetings dear friends. Thank you for being here. I was introduced to Alcoholics Anonymous out at Guest House. I was there for more than a year, and during that year we had the privilege of having a Canadian doctor come down to our place from Toronto. He would spend the whole day with us. He ran a clinic in a suburb of Toronto on various kinds of addiction including alcoholism. He wasn't an alcoholic but he would lecture to us. He was a blackboard lecturer and he was a wonderful speaker. When he spoke, he was like a man dancing. He was constantly moving. I was always amazed at the amount of subject matter he could write on a blackboard and still be legible.

I was privileged to hear him three times. He would lecture for a couple of hours. Then we would stop for a coffee break and return for some more. I'll never forget some of the things he said. The thing that comes to mind tonight is, "Recovery begins when the patient takes over." It reminds me of the words in the Fifth Chapter of The Big Book, where Bill W., writing for the membership, says, "Here is the legitimate area for the use of will power." It's a program of action. It's not a program of talking so much, although that's important, too. A lot of our recovery comes from our sharing with one another and the great communication we can have with one another as alcoholics. But he said that recovery begins when the patient takes over. We know that we don't have any power over alcohol, and we are powerless over the various aspects of the disease, at certain moments.

But there are some things that we can do. Even they may require the help of God for us to get started. But we are able to make a decision, for example, to go to meetings. We don't allow that to depend on how we feel. We recognize the fact that we need help. When we are tempted to stay home, we grab ourselves by the scruff of the neck and get to a meeting. That's will power. When we get there, we don't always feel like listening. Maybe we have other things on our mind. We're distracted, but we make an effort of will to listen. It's that way with a lot of other things. We have to take responsibility for our recovery. Along with that goes this idea of following suggestions. There are things in the steps that suggest certain courses of action—whether the action be physical, mental or spiritual, an act of the will. We go into action. This is especially difficult in the beginning. In the beginning, our progress may be so slow that it may seem to be moving at a snail's pace. We can hardly discern day by day whether we're making any progress at all. That's where faith comes in. We believe. I'm talking of believing in the experience of AA, what we hear from other people in AA. I'm also talking about believing in the Higher Power or the God of my understanding. But first of all, I'm talking about believing the old-timers who have recovered when they tell us how their recovery came about. It takes faith to stick with the program even during those moments when we feel we are going backwards or we doubt that we're making any real progress. It's something like a man trying to follow a path in the dark. We are stepping out in a kind of trusting way. We can't see really how far we're advancing, if we're advancing at all. That's when we need the help of one another and the help of God to keep moving. We have to stay in action and to keep trying these suggestions even when they don't seem to be working.

So recovery begins when the patient takes over. As the patient, when I accept some simple suggestions, and do my best to put them into practice, I'm on my way to recovery. If I stick it out long enough, after a while I experience within myself some of this recovery. In the early days, when I first began to feel a little better inside, I was afraid to look at it. I was afraid it would disappear. In the past, many things that I had tried seemed to work for awhile and then they blew up in my face. So I was afraid for a while. But as time went on in AA and the progress within me got better and stronger, I could no longer deny the fact that I was feeling better, but I began to get worried because I wasn't worrying about anything. I'm a person who identified myself by the fact that I was always worried about something. Now I'm not worrying. Who the heck am I?

We are at the Eighth Step tonight. A long time ago an old-timer told me that more than half of the program has to do with some kind of an inventory or what you do about an inventory. When I first heard it, I was a little shocked. But as I looked more closely, I thought it was true. From Step Four up to and including Step Ten, every one of the steps is about an inventory or what to do about your inventory. It helps to realize more deeply how important the inventory is. It sent me back to the advice in The Big Book, where they said, "We tried to find an easier way." They found out by experience that they had to do this inventory. And they said, "We beg you with all the earnestness at our command to be thorough."

Step Eight is sort of a continuation of the Fourth Step and the Ninth Step is sort of a continuation of the Fifth Step. When we make a Forth Step, we are looking at ourselves. We look at our entire lives, our own good points, weak points, and defects. We also look at how we have related to other people.

The Eighth Step says, "This time take a look at other people." In the Fourth Step, the emphasis was on myself. What kind of a person am I? Very necessary for us recovering alcoholics to get to know something about ourselves. In the Fifth Step we accept our faults and admit them to God, ourselves, and another human being. The Eighth Step says, "Now when you look at your story, look carefully at how you were related to other people." This is a social dimension of our lives. That doesn't mean dances and tea. How are we related to the people we lived with and worked with and met?

The Eighth Step says, "Made a list of those we had harmed." That's very simple and clear. We are to sit down and try to list the people we have harmed. Many of them will have appeared in the Fourth Step. But maybe some of them didn't occur to us when we were doing the Fourth. It doesn't say made a list of people we harmed when we were drinking. It says made a list of people we harmed. This includes people we harmed even before we began to have trouble with alcohol. That's a reality of our lives. If we harmed someone even before we were really in trouble with alcohol, that needs to be cleared up.

"Made a list of those that I have harmed." It doesn't say, made a list of those we harmed grievously or harmed to a great extent. Maybe we harmed some more than others. Of course there has to be an element of common sense to it, or it could get ridiculous. I can't track down every tiny little thing that ever happened or I'll go crazy.

I was told that I make such a list to the best of my ability and I have it on paper, that even if I were to do only that—only make a list—it would help me in some way. It would certainly help me get rid of the old alcoholic rationalization, "Leave me alone. I'm not hurting anybody but myself." An old-timer in AA told me that everybody hurts a least six other people, whether he thinks so or not. If we make this list and look at it, it helps us to appreciate the gravity of our condition. It helps us to get rid of this rationalization—"The only one I ever hurt was me." It shows us in black and white in our own writing how false that is. We see how devastating this disease is in our relationships with family, friends, and fellow workers. That can motivate us to keep going to meetings and to keep using the program to recover from this disease, so that we don't relapse and fall back into it, and fall back into this type of destructive conduct.

When I was first in AA, and I looked at the Twelve Steps, I saw this step, "Made a list of those we had harmed and became willing to make amends to them all," I thought it would be an easy one. How little I knew. When we do come to it, we find out there is liable to be some son of a gun in there who we don't like. "Made amends to them all." I can think, "It's going to be kind of difficult to make amends to him because he's not a nice guy. I don't like him."

It says that we made amends, it doesn't say that we apologize. It doesn't say, "We crawled on our hands and knees and begged for forgiveness." That might be appropriate in some instances. It says that we became willing to make amends to them all—to do whatever is possible to straighten things out.

When it comes to the Eighth and Ninth Steps, The Big Book says that these steps are designed to help us put our social relationships, friendships, companionships, and our dealings with one another on the best possible basis. That's an ideal. We become willing to make amends to do whatever can be done to straighten this situation out. There are many kinds of amends.

Many of the things we did were done when we were actively alcoholic. Even when we weren't drinking, we did not have complete knowledge and freedom. We had this personality disorder which wasn't being treated. We were sick. I'm not trying to excuse everything. I don't excuse everything in myself. But it is true that we are dealing with a three-fold disease. When this disease is not being treated—when we're not taking the medicine for recovery—we are very, very sick people. As Father Frank Dowd use to say, God rest him, "We don't realize how sick we were." I think there's a lot of truth in that. Not every harm that we did to other people was done on purpose. It was done in our sickness.

We make the proper kind of amends. If I harmed you in my sickness, when it wasn't my conscious deliberate will to harm you, I don't have to come crawling to you because I didn't do you a deliberate injury. I was the occasion and the cause of injury to you. I am willing to do whatever it is I can do to straighten it out with you so that you and I can get along together; so that as a recovering alcoholic I can meet you without feeling that I have to run away or hide from you. I'm out in the open now.

"To become willing to make amends to all of them." The step itself is universal—it says "all." That's a high goal that we're aiming at. Somewhere in The Big Book it brings out the point that by aiming at the best, we achieve something. It's like aiming an arrow from a bow, or shooting a long distance with a gun; if I aim a little above the target, I'm more likely to come near it than if I don't aim that high. In the Eighth Step we're aiming at an ideal goal. "Made a list of those we have harmed and became willing to make amends to them all."

There is another element that comes into this step. It's in The Twelve and Twelve. I was going to meetings for a long, long time before I ever noticed it. I was at a step meeting, on this step, some years ago chaired by Joe S., God rest him. He brought this element of the chapter out very well. It's only a sentence or two in the Eighth Chapter in The Twelve and Twelve. It's a suggestion that before we make a list of the people we have harmed, we make a list of the people who harmed us, and then by the grace of God, we become willing to forgive them. Forgiveness in its complete meaning is a wonderful thing. It means to let go entirely, and say to a person, "You are free, you don't owe me anything." If I can do that, then I can meet this someone who injured me and my mind doesn't begin by saying, "Oh, here's the fellow that hurt me." No. I forgave him. It's gone. "You're off the hook. You're entirely free. I hold nothing against you. I give you your freedom. And I not only forgive you, I forget it."

This amazed me because I hadn't noticed that in the step. The Book says that we find out for ourselves how difficult it is to forgive, when we have our own experience of trying to forgive. Maybe we have been holding a grudge for years against a person who harmed us. Maybe we are so used to it we don't notice it anymore. And we are brought face to face with this challenge: Can I, will I forgive this man? I've been painting a black picture of him in my imagination, maybe for years. I've written him out of the Book of Life. I've decided within myself that he has no worth at all. Can I forgive him? The Big Book says that without the spirit of forgiveness, our own recovery is blocked. That's true in other areas, including religious areas. We have it in the Our Father—which many of us say. We ask God to "forgive us our trespasses, our sins against you, as we forgive those who sin against us."

I began hearing all over the place that without the spirit of forgiveness recovery is blocked and the grace of God is blocked in my life—in a spiritual, religious way. Recently I heard in church a beautiful homily by a priest on this subject. The gist of what he said was that forgiveness is impossible to us human beings. It's so contrary to our humanity, our human nature. This deep, inveterate desire we have to get even is such that we need the help of God to forgive, to let go, forgive, drop it. "It's over. You're forgiven. I hold nothing against you." There's a suggestion in that; it's not an order, but it can be very profitable to us. The chances are we may find somebody who we are unwilling to forgive. We're back to "and became willing." How do we become willing to give this forgiveness? Well, we could think, "If I don't forgive, I'm running a danger of being stuck here. If I do forgive I'm going to be set free. That would be wonderful. But now let me ask the God of my understanding to help me." That is, I believe, a very useful part of the step. It's not in the words of the step, but it's a suggestion in the chapter.

There is another suggestion in the chapter that could take time but it seems to me that it's very helpful. When I make a list of the people I have harmed and I have it before me, I can take them one by one, if I have the time and the willingness, and I can examine what was it in me that caused me to harm this person. Here's an example. I ignored this fellow. I did it systematically. It wasn't a tragedy, but I harmed him. Why did I ignore him? I may find out it was that if I approached him and had a conversation with him that it might turn out that he is much smarter than I am. It's going to make me look a little less, or a great deal less.

The chapter says if I can find out what in me caused me to injure people in different ways, then I'm getting some more information about me and what I need to change and grow.

Look at how much is included in this step if you consider all those points. The longer I'm in the program the more I see the step. It doesn't mean that everybody has to do every little thing that is suggested here. But suppose somebody wants to use all the means available to make progress. "Here is this list of all I have harmed. Here is my study of what caused me to harm this person this way and this other person this other way. And then here's the list of the people who have harmed me—am I becoming willing to forgive them?" There's a whole business of becoming willing, of meditating, of praying, of looking around in AA and seeing the example of other people who have worked a little longer on it than I have.

We get encouragement from one another to become willing to make amends. It uses the word amends. That means all kinds of amends, whether they are indirect or direct. We'll talk about direct amends in the next step. In any other kind of amends, I don't approach the person face to face because for some reason that can't be done. In some cases I make amends by the way I live, by my fidelity to the program and recovery, by my growth as a family member, a friend, and a worker. Thanks to the program and the grace of God I am making amends by becoming a better person, a healthier, sociable, kinder person who can work with others. I'm not afraid of saying, "I love you" and of being a more complete human being.

I repeat this. The Big Book says the purpose of the Eighth and Ninth Steps is to put our social relationships in the best possible basis. None of us is ever going to be perfect in that way, but the chances are we can be a lot better than we used to be. This is one of the tools. It's not easy. It's work. It's like a doctor's prescription.

I'll close with the saying of the doctor that I started with, "Recovery begins when the patient takes over." When we use these steps, when we take over, and do what we can to put them into practice we get better and our lives get better.

I remind you once more that on Good Friday, that is the fourteenth of next month, we won't have a gathering here. The building won't be open on Good Friday night. If you know anybody who is thinking of coming here will you warn them about that?

Thank you very much for your presence and your kind attention.

# Step Nine

*"Made amends to them all."*

G ood evening everybody. I've said this two or three times, and I'll say it again. What I'm talking about here is just my own opinion, my own experience. It is by no means the last word and I don't look upon it as that. I'm just sharing with those who are willing to listen to what I think about the steps of Recovery. I know it's probably helpful to me to talk, and I hope it may be useful to someone else.

I mentioned earlier how surprised I was some years ago when an old-timer mentioned to me that more than half of the Twelve Steps have to do with an inventory or what to do with an inventory. When I had a moment of leisure, I looked at The Big Book and found out that is the truth. Seven of the twelve steps have to do with some kind of an inventory or what to do with it. That helped me, and it may help you, to appreciate the importance of this major part of our recovery program. In the Fourth Step, as I said, I think the emphasis on my inventory is about me—what kind of a person I am.

But necessarily, with all of us, other people came into that story. So, in the Fourth Step we already have the beginning of the Eighth Step list. In some cases we may have the whole Eighth Step list. In the Eighth Step, as I said before, I think the emphasis now is on the social side, the people that I affected, the people I have harmed. The Fourth Step underlines the personal and the Eighth Step underlines the social. I believe that in making this Eighth Step list of all those we have harmed, just to write down the names of those we remember that we have harmed is a very valuable help. It was impressed on me that if I did make such a list, at least I could look at it and I could get rid of the rationalization that the only one I harmed was myself. I could begin to see how destructive, how harmful my disease was to others—to my family and fellow religious and friends and people I was associated with. The harm may not always have been extreme, may not always have been grievous—though in some cases it might have been—but it certainly was a drag on them. I believed that seeing that would deepen my motivation to get more and more serious about using the program to recover from this dreadful disease. So making the list had a value even if I did nothing else except to make that list.

I found out that in my own case, in making that list, that because of my position as a priest and as a teacher, it was easier for me to harm many people at once. That made it kind of an appalling difficulty for me. For example, in the years when I was teaching or going into a classroom, I harmed my students by not being at my best or anywhere near it, by not giving them everything I should have given them. How could I keep count of all those individual persons? There were also the fellow Catholics I harmed, for example, by not being available when people might have wanted to talk to me or by conducting a prayer service when I was really drunk. When I think of that I shiver. I think of all the people that I must have harmed—maybe not to an outrageous degree but to some degree. Maybe it was really scandalous to some of them. But how could I know who they are? In the beginning, like so many others, I might have thought, "Well, I didn't harm many people." Many of us think that way. We are so self-centered and we are so wrapped up in our own hat maybe we don't think about others so much.

When we come to this step in our recovery, we begin to think more clearly about that social dimension in our lives. We think of the various kinds of harm there are. Harm can be physical. It can be financial. It can be spiritual. One area where some of us can be blind, in the beginning, is to emotional harm. In the Eighth Chapter in The Twelve and Twelve—I can't tell you the exact page right now—there is a whole page or more cataloging certain emotional harm that we alcoholics can do to our family. For example, a married man can be dominating. He can give orders and minute directions like a drill sergeant. He can scream at his children or play favorites. I think of the emotional burden I was to my own Jesuit community, even when I wasn't drinking. Even then I was still suffering from alcoholism. It was not yet understood or faced or treated or dealt with. I had a lot of depression, a lot of gloominess. As I look back, I must have been a real burden to many of my companions when I was in a mood like that. I remember that quite some time before I got to AA, a very good Jesuit friend of mine said to me, "You haven't smiled or laughed in two years." Gloom, depression, a living death, even when not drinking. How do you make amends for that?

The Eighth Step says that having made a list of those we have harmed, we become willing to make amends to them. Then if we want to, we can study each individual instance and try to learn a little more about ourselves. Why did I harm him or her in this way rather than in that way? It might increase our self knowledge. Then it says, "We became willing to make amends to them all." Becoming willing, when we reach that point, can be quite a task. There may be certain people on that list who have harmed us, too. Possibly, they have harmed us more than we have harmed them. Perhaps such individuals have never made any move towards making amends to us. We can begin thinking that way. At times, it's hard for us to come back to this point—this program is for me to recover. It's not for him or her. First, it's for me. Regardless of how this other person might treat me, in order to recover I need to become willing to make amends. In the Eighth Step it doesn't define what kind of amends. It says amends, whatever kinds possible. When we come to the Ninth Step, which we're on tonight, it says, "We made direct amends to those we have harmed except when to do so would harm them or others." We have that word "direct" amends. I have a list of people I have harmed and out of this list there are some of them to whom I can make direct amends. It would be impossible to make direct amends to some of them without causing greater harm. It's implied therefore, that I probably can't make direct amends to all the people I have harmed.

What would you call the type of amends that are not direct? I use the word indirect. Indirect amends means that by living the program and practicing its principles, by recovering, by beginning to take a responsible place in the family and in my profession and in the workshop or the classroom, by beginning to be a responsible, caring person, I'm making indirect amends. To whom? To myself, to my family, to all those around me, and I'm making amends to God. God brought me into the program, and I have offended him. By my sincere effort to live this program, and to make progress, I am indirectly saying to all the people I've harmed, to my family, to my friends, to society, and to God, "I recognize that I have a debt and by my way of life, I am trying to pay off and fulfill that debt." I look upon that as indirect amends.

When we come to the direct amends, the chapter tells us that this calls for good timing and for prudence. We hear the word prudence sometimes and we think of it as a distasteful word. We may think of it as meaning a cowardly caution. "I've got to be cautious. I can't dare to take a chance." That is not the virtue of prudence. Prudence is one of the so-called four cardinal virtues, one of the attributes of a grown-up person. It means the ability to take the right means to reach the given end. The means may be dangerous, but if they are the right means to reach the end, a prudent person takes them. Prudence here is a great virtue; that is able to see, to discern, "What's the best way to do this?" First of all—is this a situation where I can make direct amends—where it is possible and where it can be done without causing greater harm? Prudence and discernment. As The Big Book warns us, it's not an invitation to postpone it or to lag back. It's a suggestion and a warning that a lot of prudence is needed.

Good timing. I can't enumerate specifically all the instances where that would apply. This might be a very simple one: if there's somebody that I have harmed and I want to make direct amends to, but at the moment he's drunk, maybe that's not the right time to do it. Suppose he's not drunk. He's okay. But he's got a family problem. His wife is seriously ill with cancer. Is this the time? Good judgment would be needed there. All kinds of circumstances like that can come into consideration—good timing and prudence and a willingness. We're also told that before doing this, we need to make sure that we're on the right wavelength, we're on the AA beam. I'm trying to recover myself, and I find out that I have harmed this man. That's in my consciousness and it's interfering to a degree with my life. When I see that man or meet him maybe at a meeting, or at the market, or at church, or at the club, or work, I'm not comfortable with him. I know that I owe him something. My tendency is a fearful one, to avoid him. That's not good for me. It's not so good for him either. But the program is for me, first, to recover—to do what is prudently required for me to recover my standing, my health, my social health. We are told on the Ninth Step that the amends that we make should be magnanimous. It's for me first, but it is not only for me. It's for others too—including this imaginary man I'm talking about. If I decide to make amends to him, it should be done generously and even magnanimously, with a large spirit. It still remains true that the step is for me, to free me from this sort of a bondage of an unresolved problem that's interfering with my social life, and with my relationship with this person. In this regard where we are called to be prudent and to have good timing, we may also need the help of our sponsor or a counselor or friend to give us advice. But when the road is clear we should do it openly. We can't make direct amends secretly or privately. The Big Book describes a person going to the one who has been offended and telling him what it's all about. "I have offended you. I'm in a recovery program. And for my recovery, it's necessary for me to speak to you and to do whatever I can and to make direct amends to you." It's right out in the open. This is a serious matter requiring prudence and good timing and trust in God. It's clear that I'm doing this to recover myself, but I'm not saying I'm the only one that counts. I'm going to do it with a large spirit so that this person, too, may get some benefit from it. The amends might be financial. It might be money that I owe or some kind of damage that I've done to his property. It could be a thousand different things. It could even be emotional things. Precisely what form the amends are going to take is apt to be decided by the circumstances. But the spirit is there—the direct amends. It's in the open. I let the man know what I'm up to and why I'm doing it.

Suppose that my effort to make amends is rejected. That's why it's wise to be on the right beam to have proper timing. Have I been in the program long enough? Do I think I would be able, at the present time, to withstand a negative response? That comes into it, too.

I got into the program out in a recovery place in Michigan. I was out there for over a year. When I came back to Worcester, one of the first things I did was go to Boston to a Jesuit House and visit a friend of mine. He was a Jesuit who had been one of my superiors. We had been good friends, but for a few years, I had been a thorn in his side. I was eager to go and see him. When I did see him and I made my amends, much to my surprise, he said to me, "Oh, it's about time." I wasn't expecting that, but I had been in the program long enough not to let it tip me over. I think of it now—a dear friend, that's what he is, or was, he's been dead for some years—but I often think of that. Isn't that too bad.

The point is that I did what I had to do. When that was over, despite the surprising reaction on his part, at least I could say to myself, "Well, I did what I had to do." I made an effort to make amends and that was a very helpful step for me. Another experience I had was with a couple of aunts who were still living in Boston who had been very good to me. I had imposed on them dreadfully for some years during my drinking years. I hastened to them, too, to make my direct amends. What happened there? They wouldn't listen to me. Do you know what it was like? It was like expecting to walk through a door, but you find out the door isn't there and you walk into a wall. I found that the same thing happened with some other relatives of mine. My brother, for example, God rest him. I tried more than once to talk to him. He wouldn't hear me. He wouldn't listen to me. I suppose that these people who loved us were so happy that we had turned it around and were back on our feet again that they didn't want to hear anything about it. All they cared about was that we were okay. Maybe in their own minds, they minimized the condition that we had been in. Maybe it was so painful to think of their beloved nephew or brother in that shape he was in that they couldn't bear to think of it again. That might be it, too.

I learned something important from that. A few times people in the program have come to me to make amends for some thing. In my mind it was nothing. I couldn't even remember what they were referring to. Even if I could remember it, to me it was nothing. The first two or three times this happened, I reacted like my own brother or my aunts. I brushed it off. I finally realized that I shouldn't do that. This thing that seems to be of very slight importance to me is very important to them. They are doing something that they need to do for their recovery. It didn't happen too often. I have never been really injured in any serious way, as far as I know. But whenever somebody comes to me now, I listen carefully and seriously and let them say what they have to say. That's what I've learned from those incidents. But I still have in my own mind and heart and soul a sort of disappointment that these relatives who were so dear to me wouldn't let me come out with my amends. I have to accept that and know that I did all that I could.

Here's another experience. I think that this is an example of something that is said somewhere in The Big Book. It says that although the damage or the harm may be small in itself, it may have serious emotional consequences. I'm not going to go to confession with you here tonight, but I did harm to a fellow Jesuit many years ago. I looked at it. It was minor. It was a small thing. But to me, to my consciousness, it was huge. It was a least fifteen years before I got the good opportunity to make direct amends to this man who is still living. I met him somewhere, of course, and I made the direct amends. He had absolutely no recollection of what I was talking about. But that moment in my life in AA was a huge moment. It was a small matter but it wasn't small inside of me. It was galling me and it would come to the surface every now and then and I would say, "Gee, I've got to do something about that." Finally, the occasion arrived and I did it and it set me at peace.

We have all heard it mentioned often at AA meetings that sometimes even when you reach the point when you're ready to make direct amends to somebody, the opportunity just doesn't seem to be there. But if you wait and you pray, sooner or later God provides the opportunity as he did for me.

I think the part about not making direct amends if it's going to harm somebody else is very important. Of course there could be any number of different ways—that I can't enumerate now—where such harm might come about. That's where we need prudence and maybe a little advice from a sponsor. We can't expose somebody else to suffering just so we can get rid of our own suffering. Sometimes, it may be that God is asking us to bear with him, to accept the fact that we have this debt that we can't pay in this particular way, and to accept that and live with it. That may be. I'm not saying that's so in every case, but I don't see why it can't be the truth in some cases. This is a very intricate matter. I certainly don't know and can't give a list of all the different ways in which doing the direct amends might harm somebody else. But we have to be aware of that. We have to have careful timing. We can't be so anxious to get this thing done that we do it rashly and possibly at the expense of another person.

At the beginning of these two steps, the Eighth and the Ninth, we are told in The Twelve and Twelve that these steps are designed to place our personal, social relationships on the best possible basis. The best basis. Part of that basis is honesty—honestly admitting the harm done and having an honest desire to make whatever kind of amends are possible. Both of these steps are liable to be an ongoing process for a good part of our life. Even after we have done our best with an Eighth Step list, something later on may rise to our consciousness and we may remember something for the moment that we need to make amends for. But we need to be prudent and know where to cut it off. We should not become over meticulous or scrupulous, and we should not be nit-picking and making mountains out of mole hills. Where is that point? I don't know. Each one needs to pray for discernment, judgment, and prudence; also, having the help of a sponsor and following his advice can bring one to be at peace.

I think of the Ninth Step as something like the Fifth. The Eighth is like the Fourth and the Ninth is like the Fifth. We put those four steps together with these inventories of ourselves and the harms we've done to others. In the Fifth Step we admit our shortcomings to God, to ourselves, and to another human being. Then in the Ninth Step, we make amends, direct amends wherever possible. This really is a house cleaning to put it mildly.

If we just simply do these things that are suggested, what a marvelous work it is. We're encouraged to do them. We have a good sponsor and we have friends that encourage us to do them. It is a work of re-organizing ourselves and putting our relationships on the best possible basis to live happy lives. We recover our health and live productive lives—lives that make us not only happy within ourselves but useful to our family and our friends.

And once more, I thank you for listening.

# Step Ten

*"Continued to take a personal inventory, and
when we were wrong, promptly admitted it."*

Greetings everybody. Before I forget it and I think
it's been said already, next Friday night we won't
have a gathering here. It's Good Friday. It's not
because there is anything wrong with having a meeting or a
gathering on Good Friday, but the building won't be open. So
we will skip next week and then we will have three more
meetings, spending the last two on the Twelfth Step as we do
usually at step discussion meetings.

Let's just review briefly where we are by the time we
reach the Tenth Step. In the first three steps, we laid a foundation for our sobriety and continuing sobriety. We admitted
our powerlessness, we came to rely on a power outside of ourselves, and we handed our selves over to the care of a loving
Higher Power, a loving God. By living those three steps, even
though we did not do it all perfectly or near perfection, we
found out for ourselves that what it means to be sober is different from what it means to be dry.

We all know what is meant to be dry. In the last few years of my drinking, I was a bender drinker, a booze fighter. I had many relatively short periods of dryness of four or five months. Those periods of dryness were filled with tension. I strained with everything in me to stay away from the first drink. I lived with fear—the deep inside knowledge—that sooner or later this was going to break down. I was going to drink again and be in more trouble. Booze fighting—what a way to live. Then after some time in AA when I began to put the first three steps into my life, I discovered what it meant to be sober. I was staying away from a drink a day at a time not merely by my will power or even by ordinary prayer. I was relying on God to keep me away from the first drink for one day, to save me from alcoholic thinking, and to help me grow up emotionally. I put the whole kit and caboodle, my will and my life, in his two hands.

When I got some idea of that Third Step—this kind of trusting surrender into the care of God to take care of me day by day, provided I did the footwork—I began to relax. It immediately made a noticeable difference to me and to my state of health. I began to sleep a little bit better. I began to enjoy my meals a little bit. Up to this point everything was stretched taut. I was fighting, fighting, fighting.

These three steps showed me this new way of living with my three-fold illness—which is an illness of the body, the mind, and the will. You have had the same experience, I'm sure. What a discovery it is. What a blessing it is when the miracle begins to come into our life. Not only can we stay away from the first drink of alcohol for a day, but we can begin to be happy. That was the demolition of the old mythology that we had before AA—that if I can't drink at least occasionally how can I enjoy life? I found out in the program, through these three steps, that that is a lie. I found out that with the help of God, I can stay sober and I can enjoy life. I can recover with a taste for living.

So the first three steps are a foundation which needs to be renewed day by day. We can't leave them behind us. That becomes easier for us as we learn our own methods, keeping those things in us.

In the beginning we were told that if we remained the same kind of person we were before we came to AA and before we stopped drinking, that we were in danger. Things inside of us could cause us trouble. They might even be serious enough later on to expose us to the thought of drinking again. That's one side of it. The other side is more positive— it's not enough to stop drinking and to do so happily, I need to change. I need to grow. I need to get new dimensions, new horizons in my life. That was very motivating to me, when through the inventory and through what I heard in the program I began to realize what an emotional child I was. I did not want to remain a child, I wanted to grow up.

In the Fourth and Fifth Steps, we try to find out what kind of a person we are. What are our good points? What are our weak points? What are our weaknesses? What are our tendencies—our emotional distortions? There's a whole host of them—as we all know—we hear them mentioned often. The Fourth Step focuses on me. Of course it brings in other people, but I think the emphasis in the Fourth and the Fifth Steps is clearing up the wreckage inside of me. I do this with a thorough inventory which I share—by admitting it to God, to myself, and to another human being. My own opinion is that if I have done my Fourth and Fifth Steps thoroughly, I don't need to do it again. I'm free to do it again if I want to—but if I've done it thoroughly, that's it. If I haven't done it thoroughly, if I begin to have trouble or worries about it, after I talk with my sponsor I might find it advisable to do it again. It's that important. Those who stand behind The Big Book say, "We urge you with all the earnestness at our command to be thorough." They say that they tried to find an easier way, but it isn't there. Our life and our happiness and our usefulness are at stake. This is well worth doing thoroughly.

Having done the Fourth and the Fifth Steps, we now have a renewed knowledge of ourselves. We know those traits in ourselves, the weaknesses and the defects, that make life less successful, less happy, and which could even threaten our sobriety. In the Sixth and the Seventh Steps, we are willing to have God remove these defects as he removed the alcohol and the alcoholic thinking and the alcoholic self-will. We are willing to supplant them with positive qualities—with virtues—with outgoing, generous, friendly, sociable, loving, long suffering, patient traits in our character—to become more completely ourselves and to grow up. If there ever was an ongoing, daily procedure, it's the Sixth and Seventh Steps.

After those steps we have the Eighth and the Ninth which are a continuation of the Fourth and the Fifth. In the Eighth, we look at how we have affected other people in a social aspect of our illness. This helps us, first of all, to realize more deeply what a devastating illness we have and how destructive it is. We can no longer say, "Don't bother me. I'm not hurting anybody but myself." It turns that egoism upside down. It puts the ego where it belongs. We make whatever amends we can. When we have done a good job on the first nine steps we have dealt with the past.

We hear frequently in AA that the last three steps, Tenth, Eleventh, and Twelfth, are maintenance steps. The Tenth Step, which we are on tonight, is one of these maintenance steps. It's an inventory. It says, "We continued to take personal inventory and when we were wrong, promptly admitted it." The inventory in the Tenth Step deals with today. What happened today? What helps me to make today's inventory is the knowledge that I have gained from the previous inventory steps. I have learned something more about myself. If it isn't something new, I have learned it in a new way and it is clearer. I know a lot about myself. I have some idea of who I am. It's not a perfect idea of who I am. I don't believe that anybody in this life can have perfect self-knowledge. It's too difficult. But we can grow in the self-knowledge.

The Fourth Step and the Fifth Step are on-going, in the sense that the knowledge that I derive from them remains with me today. It is like a catalog of things that I need to watch. The Tenth Step is an inventory of my performance today. Some of the points that can be touched on in this inventory are how we are working the program. I could say, "How am I doing with the slogans? Am I living the Serenity Prayer?" Then I could look through the principles in the steps—the admission and acceptance of powerlessness, reliance on God, the surrender of my self-will. I could ask myself, briefly, "How am I doing? Am I keeping the program alive?" It would take us about a year maybe to do the inventory if we watched every particular, not just outlining them as possible reference points. Next, I could deal with what I know about myself—the weaknesses or the defects that I wrote down on paper and told to another man. I don't have to catalog them. You know them as well as I do—things like procrastination, selfishness, self-centeredness, fear. How often we can be afraid and be afraid to admit it. That's just a few. This inventory is to clear up today, so that I won't have an accumulation of problems in my wake as I did before I came to AA and did the Fourth Step.

Dr. Bell, who I have mentioned a few times, said that one of the best ways to find out about who you really are, is to find out how you really feel about things. It's only one of the ways but it's a good way. We can deceive ourselves. I know I can. I'll use a harmless example. Most of us grew up making a big hullabaloo about Thanksgiving. It's Thanksgiving. We're going to have a turkey. Mama's going to put the turkey in the oven, and we will all hover around, watching and asking how it's doing. To me it was make-believe. Even when I was a kid, I would just as soon have a nice juicy hamburger. I was trying to make myself feel like I felt I ought to feel—like a real American boy. Well, I don't love turkey. But I felt I ought to dance around with glee because we had turkey with all the fixings.

That's just an example. Here's another one. I'm telling a fellow off because I want to see him fly straight. But the truth is, I want to put him in his place. I want to fix that fellow. That is the underlying motive and feeling. Years ago, I got a big notebook. I would come home at the end of the day when sometimes I could hardly stand up—but I'd get this book out and I'd write down certain things. Then I'd say, "What were my real feelings about that thing?" It's awfully difficult. Maybe one reason is that I cover up. I rationalize. I pretend to be better and nobler at times than I really am. I did this for some weeks before I finally realized that if I kept this up I'd break down for lack of sleep. It takes so long to do it. But I pass it on to you as something, that if you haven't looked into it that carefully, you might like to spend a little time on questioning yourself. "How do I really feel?" I don't advocate overdoing it. We don't want to be a bunch of nuts that are centered only on ourselves. But this is a way, if you can do it a bit, to find out who you really are, where you really stand.

This Tenth Step inventory can be done in different ways. At one time I was doing it at the end of the day. I was jotting things down. When I found out that was too much for me in my particular set of circumstances, then almost automatically it became more of a spot check. That happens to many of us. As we keep going to meetings and talking with other AA members, we notice more quickly when we're wrong. Wrong to me doesn't mean only being morally wrong. It means when I'm off the beam, when I'm acting like a childish alcoholic. An example of this was a rainy night when I was driving somebody to a meeting. I shouldn't have been driving because my vision was going. I was on the wrong side of the road. My friend reminded me two or three times, "You're driving on the wrong side of the road." I was indignant towards her. Who was she to talk that way to me? To think that her life was more important than my feelings. Anyway, finally I drove over to the right side of the road. I haughtily stepped out of the car and invited her to come over and drive. By the time I walked around the car, I came to my senses. I spotted it. It's a spot check. "I'm acting like an infant. My feelings are hurt because somebody told me I'm on the wrong side of the road and I shouldn't be driving." I took it first as an insult, but then by the grace of God I came to take it as the truth. So I cleared it up. We went to the meeting. Everything was fine. The spot check—would to God I had done it more often. In the spot check, we realize this is a childish reaction. I reacted out of hurt feelings and defended myself against this fellow member. That's not sobriety. We become aware of our own conduct and we become able when we were wrong, promptly, to admit it.

Why is it so difficult for us to admit we are wrong? Even some stupid little thing of no great importance. You asked me what time it is, and I told you it's ten past ten. I find out it's eight past. I was wrong. Why is it so difficult for me to say to myself, "I was wrong." Is that a mystery?

A lot of us come to the program with this defect—we don't believe in ourselves. We have a low self-image. We bluster our way through. If somebody else says we don't amount to much, we're ready to fight. But we're saying the same thing to ourselves, inside. Maybe we're afraid that if we make a mistake, even if it's a little one, that goes to prove that we don't amount to much. We can't afford to make a mistake or if we make one, we can't afford to admit it. I think that might have been true in my own case.

This is the hard thing—first of all to admit to myself that I was wrong or that I acted in a way that wasn't grown up. I wasn't patient, wasn't kind, wasn't polite, wasn't fair, wasn't just—to admit that to myself. One reason why I like this part of the step is that I can't do that by accident. If I admit to myself that I'm wrong, I know what I'm doing. Then having done it and done it two or three times, I can say to myself, "By God, I did it and I'm making some progress."

This Tenth Step is like a thermometer we can use to gauge our progress. Have I made any progress in my own life by admitting when I'm wrong? Admitting to myself, never mind somebody else, and then promptly admitting it. I could easily rationalize, and say, "Sure I did that. But if the truth were known, in my case it really wasn't wrong." I'm trying to erase it. I'm trying to deny it. I was wrong. But what a sign of emotional growth, spiritual growth, progress in sobriety, when I can admit promptly that I was wrong. At the same time I have made enough progress to know that making a mistake doesn't mean that I'm a mistake. It doesn't mean that I'm worthless, that I'm of no account, that I'm not good. It means I'm a human being. I think that's very important—promptly admitting to myself when I'm wrong. Then of course, when the occasion calls for it, promptly to admit to another person—if my mistake has caused them any injury worth noticing. We don't want to run around as some of us used to before AA, apologizing. No, this is a real thing if I have done some harm or injury today to another person, and I reach this point of admitting to myself I was wrong. Then I use my prudent judgment. Maybe I should go to this person and make some kind of amends.

"Continued to take personal inventory..." It's about me. How am I doing? My conduct can effect other people. I believe this is the first of the three maintenance steps. After a while, most people in AA reach the point of being able to spot these things. If we are trying and we're sincere about the program and we're asking for help, I think gradually we are given clearer insight into how we are doing, what we're aiming at, and what we would like to become. There is a sentence we hear often in AA, "Emotional pain is a sign of progress." This is the step where we are going to feel pain. When we look at it and say that we were wrong and when we admit that to somebody else. But this pain is a sign that we are making progress. For this reason, Step Ten is a great blessing for us. We don't have to turn it into some kind of neurotic self-examination, putting ourselves under the screws all the time. It is just a common sense, reasonable look at how we are doing. "Have I been living the program today? Have I been making any progress with my common defects? Am I getting along better with myself? Am I now able to accept my real self, even though I make a mistake? Am I better able to get along with other people? If I do something that might be annoying or harmful to them, have I grown enough to make some kind of amends and not let that thing hang over my head and cause me to be gloomy or troubled, to be unfree?" To become free, to become a real person, worth—how can we say how much a human being is worth, only God can say that—worth so much and yet human and an alcoholic. I'm a recovering alcoholic. I can make mistakes. But God help me. Please help me, dear Lord, that when I'm wrong to promptly admit it to myself, and when the need is there, to admit it to another person.

And with that I'll close.

Thank you for your kind attention.

# Step Eleven

*"Sought through prayer and meditation to improve our conscious contact with God as we understood him, praying only for knowledge of his will for us and power to carry that out."*

The Eleventh Step is commonly called the second of the three maintenance steps. Those steps at the end of the program—the Tenth, Eleventh and Twelfth Steps—are designed to help the recovering alcoholic to maintain his sobriety and even to grow in his recovery. The Eleventh Step may be divided into three parts. The first part is "sought through prayer and meditation to improve our conscious contact with God as we understand him." The second part picks up the word prayer, "Praying only for knowledge of his will for us." And the third part, stays with the word "praying" as we seek the power to carry his will out.

The first part talks about improving our conscious contact with God. That assumes that we already have some kind of a contact with God. That contact happens for anybody who comes to the program and follows the suggestions. For example, the suggestion that we all heard in the beginning, to ask God, or a power greater than ourselves, to keep us away from one drink for one day. Although at the moment, some of us might have looked upon that as a mere suggestion, having nothing spiritual about it, actually it was a suggestion of prayer. We used the prayer of petition, the prayer of asking. We asked the power greater than ourselves to start us on the road of recovery and to maintain us on that road by keeping us away from one drink for one day. Then it was suggested to us that if we had success for that day, we would finish the day by thanking God for having given us a day of sobriety.

Right from the very beginning, the program was dealing with God or a Higher Power, even for people who might have been alienated from their religion, or who might never have belonged to a religion. It was prayer. It was asking to be kept away from a drink for a day and thanking God at night—the prayer of petition and the prayer of thanksgiving. As we went through the rest of the steps, we continued to need the help of God, and we asked for it as each one came up. As a result of those steps we found ourselves in some kind of conscious contact with God. That contact comes first of all through this miracle of sobriety. We advance beyond mere physical sobriety to mental, emotional, and even spiritual sobriety and serenity, and a sense of well being. In the days before AA, we were never able to bring about, by our own energy or power, the miracle of this within us.

Sobriety is like the burning bush. God appeared to Moses in the form of a burning bush and gave Moses orders so that he could accomplish what God wanted. Daily sobriety is the burning bush that is within me. It gives me an unusual experience of the power of God in my life. Remember, he is the only one I asked for this gift of sobriety.

The wonderful part of recovery is what we call a conscious contact with God. This step begins by saying, "We sought through prayer and meditation to improve our conscious contact with God." It's as if the step is saying, "This experience is so wonderful, why not deliberately go out and make a special daily effort, not only to maintain it, but to improve it, to make it even better. The means that are suggested are prayer and meditation. The very first word of the step is "sought." "Sought through prayer and meditation." To me this is significant. What are we doing here? We are human beings who are seeking happiness. In the light of my faith, what we are really seeking is God. He is the only one that can give us the wonderful happiness that our soul longs for. We are seekers. We seek day by day. We set aside a certain part of the day to give to God, to be present to God, to be in his presence. We isolate ourselves, and we are alone with the God of our understanding.

There are many books written about the distinction between prayer and meditation, but basically it's simple. Both of them are forms of prayer, but meditation is thinking about God prayerfully. It could be thinking about my recovery in the light of God's help. It could be thinking about my recovery in the light of gratitude which is so important to us recovering alcoholics—gratitude to the God who has been hearing my prayer.

Prayer and mediation: prayer is talking with God prayerfully, and meditation is thinking about God prayerfully. I don't think there is any need to try to give long-winded definitions and descriptions of the difference—it's all prayer. Each one of us prays in our own way—the way the Lord leads us and guides us. We seek him daily. That means setting aside a part of the day for this kind of prayer. It's different from what many of us might think of as our morning prayers or night prayers. It's different from the readings we might do in The Big Book or in the "Twenty Four Hour Book." This is a period in my day just for God. Some days it's very difficult. The mind is terribly distracted. It happens to everybody. But we stay there anyway for the stipulated time. It might be fifteen minutes. It might be twenty minutes, half an hour, whatever the individual can afford. It's important to stand by it day by day and to do it day after day. In the times we are distracted and we can hardly be aware of the presence of God, it's important to stay there anyway.

As I mentioned during an earlier talk, some years ago I attended a meeting with over 300 priests. A priest who was not in the program but who was a "Big Book" in the spiritual life talked to us about prayer. One of the things he said has been helpful to me. All of us, when we try to pray find occasions when we're completely distracted and feel far removed from God. On those occasions, we are liable to feel that we have wasted our time—or an hour—or fifteen minutes. But he said, "Why not waste time with God?" I think of all the times in my life I've wasted time with myself or with friends. When I was growing up sometimes I would just be with pals. We wouldn't talk about anything. We were happy to be together. As far as anything like intellectual conversation, it wasn't there. It was a waste of time in that regard. But it was wasting time with people that you loved and that loved you. That can be very helpful, even if that's the best I can do. I can say, "Well here goes, Lord. I'm going to waste fifteen more minutes, but I'm going to waste them with you."

This preamble to the Eleventh Step could also be a preamble to the Third Step, once we've gotten this far. It says one of the fruits of this prayer, of this growing conscious contact with God, is a greater strength—mentally and emotionally. As The Book says, this is the first part of recovery. It brings us closer to emotional balance, and peace of mind and serenity. In a higher order, it also makes us more capable and more ready to do God's will.

I know that when I was new in the program—the first half year or so—I had the Third Step confused with the Eleventh. I thought, back in those days, that the Third Step was saying something like this to me, "Now listen, now that you're not drinking, you're going to meetings, and coming along slowly in the program, why don't you make a decision to do God's will perfectly?" I knew that I couldn't make that promise. I felt that I could promise to do God's will in big things. I'm not kicking over the traces in big things, but it's the little things. I thought, for example, of one of the rules in religious life that has to do with obedience. When the bell rings for lunch, for example, we should stop doing whatever we are doing and answer the bell. That bell represents what God wants us to do now. It's not a sin if a religious doesn't do it, but it's a lack of that perfection that we ought to be striving for. So I thought of things like that and I said, "Gee, I can't promise that."

I was kind of hung up until I spoke my little confused piece about the Third Step at a step meeting one night. Then a man held up a little yellow pamphlet that described the steps. He pointed to the Third Step and said to me, "It says the care of God." I looked at my own book and I saw that he was right. I had not even been reading this step correctly up to that point. It says, "Made a decision to put my will and my life in the care of God." That means to me to accept the way God is taking care of me.

How is he taking care of me? Well, he's letting things happen to me. Some of the things he has allowed to happen to me are things that I can't change. He didn't cause me to be an alcoholic, but he allowed it. He allowed me to be a person who has no power over alcohol. He allowed me to be a person whom he helped to stay sober. He allowed me to be a person who needs meetings and the help and encouragement of the fellowship and what it teaches. That's what God is allowing for me. Am I willing to go along with that—and a whole lot of other things in my life, especially things that happened in the past, when I was drinking?

I was at an Eighth Step meeting last night and I remembered an incident that happened five or six years before I got to AA. At the time, I was still a booze fighter, but I had many dry periods. I used to help out in a little church in Connecticut. I went down there one Wednesday in Lent to lead the stations of the Cross. In doing the stations, a priest makes the rounds of the Church with a couple of altar boys and stops at one of fourteen stations of the Passion of Christ. He says a few prayers at each station. I was drunk. I was staggering. My speech was mumbled and jumbled. The memory of it makes me shiver when I think of it—to do that to those people and to injure myself, to offend God, to injure the priesthood. But that happened, and God allowed it to happen and I can't change it. So the Third Step is acceptance. Stop fighting it. Stop trying to change things you can't change.

God knows what he's doing. Then the rest of the Serenity Prayer—dealing with the things that can be changed—I'm supposed to go to work with God's help and the help of the program to try to change them. The Third Step has to do with Divine Providence, the way God takes care of us. He created us out of nothing, and he loves us, and he takes care of us in a most astonishing way. Sometimes he lets us get into trouble, so that we will turn to him, and I will beg for his mercy and reach out lovingly to him, and when we do, he will rescue us.

The Third Step has to do with God's care, but the Eleventh Step has to do with God's will. It says, "Praying only for knowledge of his will." What do you want me to do? This is another matter. The Third Step is what he is doing to me or allowing to happen to me. At this point in my recovery, at the Third Step point, I can put myself in his care just as I am. Even if I have a lot of baggage—faults and habits that are very wrong. Even though I'm far from being a saint—I'm sick but I'm also a sinner—I can put myself in his care. That takes an awful lot of courage because if I have any faith at all and any understanding, I know that he is going to change me. At this point I might want to hang on to some of these things that give me a perverse reward or pleasure, as The Book says.

The Eleventh Step is way beyond that. It's as though it were to say to us, "You have been living the foundation of the program, the first three steps, and you have really done a good job on the steps between the third and this. Maybe now you're ready to do what God wants you to do." You are already doing a lot of it. You're going to meetings. You're working on you're recovery. By this time many people have straightened out their life with God. Some have even gone back to the church of their childhood. Now we want to know, "What do you want me to do?" What a prayer that is. This has to do with God's will for me.

The image of God in the Third Step could be that of a life saver on a beach. I go in swimming and when I'm out a hundred yards or so and I get a cramp and I cry out for help. The life guard comes out in his little row boat. He doesn't stop and pull out a social worker's chart with my name, address, and religion. He doesn't interrogate me. "When's the last time you beat your wife? When's the last time you broke the Ten Commandments?" Not at all. He knows all about that. He's not interested. I could be one of the ten most wanted men in the country. All he wants to know at that point is, "Do you want me to help you into the shore?" That's the first question. The second question is, "Will you let me do it my way? Will you stop telling me how to do it? Will you stop grabbing me around the neck? Will you let me grab you and pull you onto shore?" If I were to say—this is kind of fantastic—"Well, on second thought, don't bother with me. I'm no damn good. Go and save that old gentlemen up there. He's worth something, but I'm no good. Just let me drown." We've felt that way at times. I know I did. It's self-hatred. So the life guard says, "Now listen. Stop that nonsense. If you let me pull you into shore, you can survive, you can be saved. And if you stay alive and if you stay in this program, later on if you want, you can become good. You can do God's will."

I picture the Lord in the Eleventh Step as my commanding officer. I stand before him in the morning, and I salute and I say, "Captain, what are the orders for today? What do you want me to do today?" So that's like the Eleventh Step. In my cultivation of prayer and meditation to improve my conscious contact with God, I'm asking him, "Lord, what do you want me to do today?" Most of us already know a great deal about what God wants us to do, just by the way we've been brought up. But here the knowledge that can come to us is a new and deeper knowledge. It's the kind of a knowledge that will make us desire to do better and to do what God wants us to do. First of all, it will make us want to achieve the highest degree of sobriety. Even this step is first of all for our recovery. It's not first of all to become the good Christian. I'm not opposed to be becoming a good Christian but the step in my opinion is for recovery. If you do this you're going to achieve a higher degree of sobriety. Incidentally, if you do it, you'll be becoming a better person too. You may even become a saint. You might even become a mystic. But the first motive here is recovery.

I've found those images help me to keep these two steps distinct. Distinct means one is not the other. They are intimately related, but one is not the other. Praying for knowledge of his will for me will be new light on what I know to be old obligations. It may be new light on my state of life—what I should do at this moment in my recovery. For example— should I start a new AA group? Or should I go back to school? It even could be, should I get married? Is that your will for me? You might say that some of it is personal and some of it is social. What do you want me to do? The only way that we are going to get light, or the main way, is through prayer. In this quiet time of being with God and asking him, some how or other he will enlighten us and guide us to what he wants us to do today. We're all the same. Most of us know certain things that God wants us to do, but we're not quite ready to do them—or we're afraid to try. Or we say to ourselves, "If I ever gave that up, how could I ever be happy again?"

Remember before we came to AA, when we were pondering the question, "Should I stop drinking? Could I live a life, even a day at a time, without alcohol?" It's easy for me anyway to remember the days or the moments when I would have said absolutely, "No, I can't. I can give it up for long periods but I can't give it up totally. It's impossible." That was my attitude when I first came to AA but I kept coming. I kept trying to do what was suggested and I finally reached a point where I experienced the real miracle of being happy in AA without a drink. It's not only going without a drink. It's doing it with serenity and with happiness and being able to find happiness in the ordinary things of life that used to give us pleasure and joy before we got sick. Some of these other things can cling to us and interfere with our happiness or recovery. I remember reading an old spiritual writer who said, "For fear of being miserable, we cling to our misery." Alcohol was making me miserable every time that I tried it—

towards the end, anyway. There was a long period where I never even got the initial lift from the first drink after a period of dryness. But once I took the first drink, after a period of dryness, I couldn't stop. And there was absolutely no pleasure. It was just sickness. But the thought of giving it up forever was too much for me. I knew that it was making me miserable, but I'd think, "How miserable I would be if I gave it up." For fear of being miserable we cling to our misery. That can happen to us with other matters in our lives where we need the light of God's will, and especially, we need the power. We need his grace to strengthen our will and to toughen us up and to give us the courage to try it and rely on him.

I don't know why this thing stayed in my memory, maybe it was providential. Years ago when I was studying theology, a professor asked the class, "What is peace of mind?" And his answer was, "Peace of mind is conformity with the known will of God." That takes in the Third Step and the Eleventh in terms of the program. If I am accepting—accepting doesn't necessarily mean approving of, or clapping my hands about it—but if I'm accepting the things in my life that can't be changed, I have peace. That means recognizing that it is God who is allowing these things in my life. He's taking care of me—as strange as it sounds. If I can accept what God is doing in my life, and if I can keep trying to know his will and get the grace to do it—to try to do it—then I have the consciousness that I'm accepting his care. I'm doing his will the best I can for the present moment, and I have peace. I have conformity with the known will of God. That's peace. Is that the same thing as what the program means by serenity? I've never been able to make up my mind, but I think they're pretty much the same. To say the same thing a different way, there is a prayer you probably have heard, "May God's will be done in me and by me." "In me" refers to the Third Step. It's God who is allowing these things and fashioning me according to his desires by the things that he allows to happen to me and by the way I react to them. Whether I react with acceptance and trust, a filial trust in his care for me, or whether I act with resentment and self-pity, and I'm boiling with anger and tension—the absolute contrary or contradiction of serenity or peace. If I am accepting God's care for me, his providence in my life and with his grace I'm doing what I know he wants me to do and I have peace.

In the life of Saint Paul, after he was converted by the apparition of the risen Christ on the road to Damascus, God reached out to this chosen vessel, something like he reached out to each one of us recovering alcoholics at some point, and said, "Come on. Come follow me." God had appointed a man in the city of Damascus, named Ananias who was to baptize Saul—that was Paul's name before he was baptized. Ananias was horrified. He said, "Lord this is the man who has been persecuting your disciples and throwing them into jail." And the Lord said, "I know, but I'm going to show him what things he will suffer in my name." There's the Third Step, suffer, things he will undergo—not things he will do, but things that will happen to him, and he will accept them in the Lord's name. Then later on the Lord said to Ananias, "I'm going to show this man what things he will do in my name." There are some occasions in the Epistles where St. Paul has to prove to his congregation that he is a real apostle, and he enumerates his suffering. He talks about the number of times he was beaten with rods, the number of times he was thrown into jail, the number of times he was naked, he was hungry, he was thirsty, he was cast up on an island, shipwrecked—a whole list of the things that he has accepted as the care of God. These things sometimes consumed a lot of time. He was on the island of Malta for two years. He was trying to get to Rome and I think that it was a storm that drove him onto the island. He was there for two years before he could get from Malta over to the mainland. It's not only the physical suffering, but it's this awful waiting that we alcoholics find is a terrible burden. Paul would enumerate these sufferings not in a spirit of self-pity or resentment but to prove to the people he was talking to that he was one of the Apostles. "I carry the mark of Christ in my body. I'm his apostle." As for the other part of it—"I'm going to show this man what he will do," that is chronicled throughout The Acts of the Apostles: the three missionary journeys, all the churches that Paul founded throughout Asia Minor and then over to Macedonia and to Greece and eventually to Rome where finally he was martyred. He had peace, but he didn't have a soft life. He had plenty of sufferings. He had plenty of grievances, but he wasn't a grieved man. He wasn't going around feeling sorry for himself. He was rejoicing in the Lord. To me that is a religious and supernatural expression of the content of the Third and the Eleventh Step. Made a decision to put my will and my life—the way I want things—and my life from day number one down to the very end—in your care. Do with me what you will, Lord, and give me the grace to accept your care and to rejoice in your love. And then in the Eleventh Step show me what you want me to do. Make your will clear to me, Lord, in prayer and give me the strength, the power to carry it out.

In the second and third part of the Eleventh Step, we find an expression of what has been formally taught in Christian circles about grace. It's called actual grace. It's a gift, a supernatural gift of God that enlightens the mind and strengthens the will—the two main powers of the soul—the knowing power and the choosing power. With this Eleventh Step there is tremendous challenge. First of all on the basis of recovery, the only way to get this peace of mind is conformity with the known will of God—to accept what he is doing and allowing, "Thy will be done in me," and doing what I know he wants me to do.

This step is really a big one. To go back to the first part of it, the more we get into prayer, and the more we improve our conscious contact with God, and the closer our daily union with God, the easier it is to do the Third Step. The easier it is to say, "Thy will be done in me." Just as in the Eleventh Step, it's the only thing that is going to give us this special knowledge and power to do the difficult thing. We know that in the whole program, we have to rely on God. And we rely on one another. We go to meetings and talk to one another. We listen to one another and we encourage one another. What a God-given program it is. We get together and by sharing with one another our experience, our strength and our hope, bit by bit, as long as we will, we get better and keep getting better and better, day by day.

And that's what I have to say on the Eleventh Step.

Thank you.

# Step Twelve

## *Part One*

*"Having had a spiritual awakening as the result of these steps, we carried this message to others and we tried to practice these principles in all our affairs."*

Greetings, greetings, greetings. Well, as Gerry said, this is the first of the last two get-togethers on the Twelfth Step. We've patiently gone through the steps, week after week, and now we are near the conclusion. Once more, I want to make it clear that I know I am speaking my own opinion. I hope that whatever I say may be beneficial to somebody, at least to myself. I'm very happy to be here. I wouldn't be here at all if it were not for the Twelve Steps of the AA program. I think I would have been dead a long time ago from this damnable disease of alcoholism. So I have to be grateful to be here. I can just barely see a couple of people in the front row, and I can't see anybody beyond them. I don't say that with any self-pity. I know that you're here and that I'm with fellow members, people who have experienced what I have, and people who have experienced the power of these steps to bring about recovery. I know that I'm with my own people and that it's the goodness of God that brings all of us

137

here together. I also believe, as you believe, that he has the power to draw good out of the efforts that we make. Our efforts may be weak or they may be strong at times, but his strength never waivers. He is the power who gives us this wonderful gift of sobriety—on the condition that we trust him and we do what we can with his help day by day. So I'm very happy to be here. I am fortunate to be here. I am blessed to be here.

The chapter on the Twelfth Step in The Twelve and Twelve begins with the sentiment, that the joy of living is the theme of AA's Twelve Steps. I contrast that with the feelings that we have before we get to AA. When I was in the throes of my own alcoholism, it was the complete opposite to joy. It was gloom. It was something close to despair. I know that by the grace of God I never lost my religious faith, and I never lost my trust in the mercy of God. But I lost my hope that God would give me any more chances. I felt I had misused or failed to use so many beautiful graces that he gave me, that I proved my unfaithfulness to grace time after time after time, and I felt inwardly convinced that I would never be set on my feet again in this life—that I would never again be happy or experience anything like joy. At the same time, I believed that in the infinite mercy of my God he might save me at the last moment from eternal loss. That was my faith and the way I felt. I didn't want to live and I was afraid to die—like "old man river." I often thought about suicide. I am not sure how deep or powerful it was. I suspect it wasn't all that terribly deep. But I believed that if it continued it might get deeper.

That was my state of mind when I came to AA. I felt that my life was over and that I was a walking scarecrow. There was nothing inside my black coat and my Roman collar. I was a spindly structure that you could hang a coat and hat on, but there was nothing inside me.

I came to the program without really believing that it would work for me. But since there was nothing else to do I tried it. As time passed I began to change, and I finally reached a point where I began to feel joy in living. That to me is one type of spiritual awakening. It wasn't, necessarily, a religious one, although it might have been related to it. It was an awakening of whatever is inside of me. I can't see it, but it is causing me to live and enables me to think and to love and to labor and to now feel that I can become a part of something. That's spiritual, but it isn't necessarily religious. It's my spirit. Another way of saying the same thing, is that bit by bit I become sober.

The word "sober" is a word that can be understood on different levels. The first level is simply not to have alcohol in my system. That is a wonderful thing. It's a miracle for me. And if I maintain that state of the absence of alcohol in me, necessarily I begin to function in my job a little better. The higher meaning of the same word "sober" is that I'm not only free of alcohol, I'm not only reasonably able to function in my job, but I'm changing inside. My way of thinking, my way of feeling, my way of deciding is changing. I'm becoming a little bit less haphazard and excited, a little bit more orderly, a little bit more serene. So it's not only in my alcohol-free body, but it is also in my mind which is clearing up. My emotions are beginning to settle down. I become aware of my self-centeredness and my self-will. And with the help of the steps of the program, change begins. Something is happening to me so gradually that many times I don't notice it.

In the early days when someone would tell me that they thought I was looking better, I would dismiss it. I would think that the person was being nice and was trying to encourage me. But deep down I didn't think that what he was saying could be true. After years of alcoholism, I had pegged myself as a futile person who can't get anywhere. But as time went on, these minute changes mounted up, and I could no longer deny to myself, something was better inside of me. I felt better.

To me, that is a part of the spiritual awakening. The inner part of me that gives life to my body and my brain, that spiritual part is beginning to work again. I'm beginning to become a human being again. I'm beginning to know what's going on around me and to be able to associate a little better with my fellow members and my friends. I am waking up inside.

When I went out to Guest House, I didn't sleep for the first four months. I didn't sleep at all. I had been going to a doctor for about three years—the tail end of my active alcoholism. I was on a couple of different kinds of pills. One was a tranquilizer to bring me down and another had a little bit of speed in it to bring me up. I also had another medication for muscle spasms, which I found out later was mood changing. I was afraid of them, and when I would see the doctor, I'd tell him that. He'd get a little angry and ask, "Who's the doctor? You or me?" Well, I was a bender drinker, and when I went on a bender I would stop taking these pills. I went on some long benders. I took the pills over a three-year period, but there were many interruptions. The director of Guest House asked me the very first night if I had medication. When I said it was in my suitcase, he told me to go and get it. I got three bottles and I gave them to him. I haven't taken any of them since. But I didn't sleep. I tried it for about a month, but finally I gave up and got myself a little radio. I would go to my room at the end of the day, after a meeting, and turn the radio softly to an all night station and sit down and write letters all night. I wrote some masterpieces! I haven't written one since. Thirteen pages of immortal prose.

Toward the end of the third month, I began to hear what was going on outside. I could hear the cries of little animals and the wind blowing in the trees. My senses were coming alive, and I was becoming open to the world around me. My mind finally began to pay attention. I would hear a little animal in trouble or the strong wind. Isn't it wonderful to discover things like that! We get in contact with reality again. That's a part of the spiritual awakening. It isn't the same thing as going to church and kneeling down and meditating for an hour. That's spiritual, too, but that's spiritual and religious. I'm not against it, you know. But first I had to wake up inside.

The first time I read in The Big Book that the alcoholic is a person who needs to rejoin the human race, I thought it was a high blown piece of rhetoric—an extreme overstatement. As I went along and I woke up spiritually, and I began to understand what I was reading, I saw that this is the literal truth about an alcoholic. One of the spiritual experiences that we had as active alcoholics is separateness or aloneness. How many times have we heard from other members that they felt alone even when they were in a crowd. They were isolated. It's like looking at life through a plate glass window. There are people out there, but we can't touch them. We can only look. That's a state of solitude. That's not necessarily a religious state. We have the experience of being separated from human beings by God knows what. We didn't understand it at the time.

The spiritual awakening is first of all, the restoration of health. It is the coming alive of something inside of me that has been knocked into unconsciousness by blow after blow of alcohol or drugs or both.

Before I admitted in the First Step that I was powerless over alcohol, I used to think—and I'm sure you can identify with this before AA—that I wasn't powerless over alcohol, I just had some bad luck. It could have been the way I was feeling or what somebody said to me. I believed that was why I got drunk. I was denying the truth about me that I cannot control alcohol. That's a state of mind—a part of the obsession, the mental part of this disease. I had a conviction that I could handle alcohol. Each time, I thought it would be different.

I came into the program and did a lot of work in the First Step. I went to meetings and listened to old-timers and did an inventory, and after a few months I finally woke up. I had a spiritual awakening in my intellect and I began to recognize that it was true that I cannot control alcohol.

Where would any of us alcoholics be tonight if we hadn't had such a spiritual awakening? That is a coming alive of our minds which tells us a basic truth about ourselves. We are powerless over alcohol. That is the beginning of a spiritual awakening.

The next aspect of this spiritual awakening happened when I finally realized from the Third Chapter of The Big Book that I am mentally powerless over alcohol as well as being physically powerless. The last paragraph in the chapter says that the alcoholic is a person who at certain moments—it doesn't say always—has no effective mental defense against the first drink. I had read that paragraph any number of times, and then I read it, and the light went on. A spiritual awakening. I saw that it meant me. This was a further meaning of my disease—I cannot continue to stay away from the first drink by my own thinking. It will help me sometimes, but there will come a time when no matter what motive comes to mind, not one of them will work against the first drink. I am capable of conning myself into picking up the first drink and triggering off the obsession and compulsion. That's another aspect of an awakening. My mind is becoming awake to the reality of my situation.

Next was the discovery, which came quite a bit later, that I was the person minutely described in The Big Book on pages sixty to sixty-four. I am that self-centered, self-willed person. My former concept of myself as a reasonable, modest fellow, easy to get along with and so forth, was a false picture. The Big Book's description of me is a much better description, pages sixty to sixty-four—Father Fred managing the universe! What an awakening. That's me. That's a spiritual awakening. It isn't that my bodily muscles became aware of it. It's my mind, my spirit. And as painful as that is, isn't it a relief when we see the truth about ourselves? Maybe not in the beginning. Who is it that says the truth will make you free but first it will make you miserable? The truth made me miserable. Is that the kind of curmudgeon I am? Wanting to have my own way and in a sneaky way, too. It's insidious. Driven all the time by this insane idea that I know what's best for me and for you. When I saw that, it was an advance and a spiritual awakening. It's like coming out of a deep sleep. The awareness grows slowly until you are finally fully awake, and you know that you're awake. Some of us never know. Or we can have days when we don't know. But awareness increases with each step as we go through the program. We find out the truth. We not only find it out, but we admit and accept it.

We are different persons. Even before we have done much of anything else, just to have those changes come about in us. This vision and acceptance of the truth about me is a spiritual awakening.

As we go along, our original concept of the steps change. In the beginning, I would look at the steps and they would seem so simple. And I would say to myself, "You mean to say that those stupid, simple things are going to get me out of the inside mess that I'm in." I felt that I was closed into a big ball of barbed wire. It represented the ten thousand problems that I had and that were going to stop me from ever getting free to live again. "You mean to tell me that those stupid little things are going to change this and set me free and got me out of this ball of barbed wire?"

If we do them, we have another awakening. We find out that they work. How often do we hear at meetings that this program works? That's an awakening. Think of all the people, maybe millions of them out there, that don't see that and don't believe it. They're the way we were at one time. They're hopeless. They have no vision and no way out of the mess they're in. But we have it. That's part of the spiritual awakening.

Now I don't want to exclude awakening to the power of God as part of the spiritual awakening. After all we are usually asking him to help us. But in the beginning, the awakening is not so much an awakening to God as an awakening to myself, to what is going on and to what is wrong and what I can do about it.

As we go along, we recover our natural health. You could call that complete sobriety. I'm free of alcohol, and I'm free of alcoholic thinking. I have grown, and bit by bit I'm getting out of the drivers seat and letting somebody else run the show. I'm becoming more able to cooperate with other people. I no longer have this deep-seated conviction, that may be spoken or unspoken, that I'm the only one in this group who really knows how to do this.

As I recover my natural health, I become the way a human being ought to be. I have a religious faith and I want to make progress in it. I am more capable of serving the God of my faith, of my church, of my religion. I have the basis of an increasing natural health, and I become more able to accept the offerings that are coming to me from God. We call them graces. Now, I am able to unite my healthy self more and more with him. That fills a void and gives me a reason to live.

What am I going to do with my new health? Will it be enough to have it written on my gravestone, "Here lies Father Fred. He died very healthy."

That is not enough for a human being. I want God. I'm talking about me now. I want to be able to come to know and to love and to serve that God in this life. That is a spiritual awakening that is also religious.

That's up to the individual. Many people, perhaps most people in AA, grow in that area too, and their lives take on a real meaning.

A book I read some years ago comes to mind. I'm sure many of you have read it, too. It was by the Viennese psychiatrist, Viktor Frankl. He spent a couple of years in one of Hitler's concentration camps, and he studied the people around him. He noticed that certain of these persecuted people were better able to stand up against the suffering and the degradation that was heaped on them, than others. And at closer study he discovered that these were the people who had a meaning or reason for living. They were able to stand up against the onslaught of these terrible persecutions and sufferings and even death itself.

This is open-ended growth. You can go as high as you want with the grace of God. It's up to the individual. But it begins with an awakening, a restoration of natural health.

Gerry said as he opened this get-together, that he often wondered how you can divide into two, a step that seems to have three clauses. And that puzzled me, too, for a long time. And I think I have the answer. It takes a genius like me!

The three clauses are—"having had a spiritual awakening as the result of these steps" that's the first clause; the second, "We tried to carry this message to other alcoholics"; and in the third clause, we repeat the word "tried," "we tried to practice these principles in all our affairs."

It's only about a year since this powerful intellect came awake to the fact that of the three clauses only two of them are suggestions! The first part is not a suggestion. It's a description of something that presumably has happened to a person who has tried to practice these steps. "Having had a spiritual awakening as the result of these steps." That's like a prelude. So having had that, then try this and try that. That's two things. You could have a meeting on trying to carry this message and another one on trying to practice these principles. But you have to use time to talk about this prelude. Another way of dividing it would be to have a meeting on the prelude— the spiritual awakening—and then have another meeting on the two suggestions—carrying the message and practicing these principles.

Quite a while ago, we used to have a Wednesday morning step discussion meeting at Austin Street. We started it to accommodate people who couldn't make it at night. There were a number of mothers, homemakers, who would get their children off to school and then come for an hour or so. One morning we had two lady visitors from New York who were old-timers in AA. We were on this step, and one of these ladies pointed out the importance of that little word, "the." "Having had a spiritual awakening as the result of these steps." I had never noticed it that carefully before. The spiritual awakening is connected directly to the practice of these steps. Not some other steps, but these that are written down. It's like a guarantee. If anybody practices these steps day by day, something happens to him that can be called a spiritual awakening. To me that was very important. There can be other awakenings from other sources.

At that time, I was fairly new in AA, but I got the great pleasure of hearing Bill W. speak at a convention in New York for members of the clergy who were in AA. It was the only time I ever saw him or heard him. I've never forgotten his talk or his manner. I can still see him. He was a tall, rather slender man, and he spoke very deliberately and thoughtfully. He talked about that spiritual experience that he had lying in that hospital in New York and what led up to it.

On an Easter morning before he wound up in the hospital, his old drinking friend, Ebby Thatcher, visited him in his apartment. Bill was sitting there with a bottle of gin on the table when Ebby came in all dressed up. Bill invited him to have a drink. But Ebby refused. Ebby told Bill that he had joined the Oxford movement. That was a movement within the English Church that stressed what they call the four absolutes. It was a religious movement.

Ebby wasn't drinking and he looked like a million dollars. Maybe he was the one who carried the message to Bill. Later on, after another bender, Bill wound up in a hospital. I know you have all read about it, and he had some kind of an experience that got him started on the road to sobriety. He talked about that experience. He said he didn't know whether it was supernatural, religious, or whether it was just some kind of a psychological event. He wasn't sure.

I don't know how it is nowadays, but you used to hear so much about that experience in and around the program and read about it, that I began to think that it might be misleading to some people. They could think that to come into AA and have this spiritual awakening, means to have some kind of a religious experience of God like St. Paul or like some other great characters like Moses who was in the presence of Almighty God. Bill's description of his experience gives the impression it was something like that. So people like you and me, ordinary run-of-the-mill alcoholics, could get the idea that we have to have some kind of a lofty religious experience. But that isn't true. The grace of God has come to each one of us. Probably we didn't know it was there. But it was

God's goodness that led each one of us into this program. Maybe there are very few if any here who have also had some great religious experience. I don't deny this possibility. But the one we are interested in is, "Having had a spiritual awakening as the results of these steps." I often wondered, did Bill write about that? What was his experience with the Twelve Steps? He must have somewhere. It's the result of these steps, not changing the program, but doing what is suggested.

Another truth that comes to us after a while, is that action is the magic word. It's by doing what is suggested that we come to understand it. I remember when I was at Guest House with about fifteen or twenty other alcoholic priests, who were trying to get straightened out in the program, Austin Ripley, the director, would often say to us, "Put your theology books on the shelf." He wasn't condemning theology. But this is not an intellectual thing. This disease yields to practice and action. We have to be beaten down. We have to be docile enough, hurting enough to be willing to do certain things, even though we don't think too highly of them. We may even think they're stupid. But we have to go ahead and do it. He used to tell us to have faith like a little child. Faith in what? Faith in the old-timers, in their experience. It's a program of experience. Have faith in their experience. And if you want to get where they are or somewhere like it, do, do, do. And that is a principle of AA—action. Action is the magic word. Do the thing and after you've done it you will begin to understand it. So I think perhaps I've talked long enough for this first get together. God willing and with your prayers and help next week we'll conclude the second half of the Twelfth Step which includes two thirds of the three clauses!

So thank you once again for being here. Thank you.

# Step Twelve
## *Part Two*

Greetings to you all. I was just thinking that a part of my spiritual awakening, is to dare to get up here and try to talk about this enormous subject matter tonight. I don't know whether that's progress or just becoming hardened. I will do the best I can to say the things I have to say and hope that they may be useful, at least to myself.

One day, when I was twenty years old and in my first year of classical studies in the Jesuit order, I pulled down from the library shelf a book of essays by a Catholic English poet named Francis Thompson. I knew a little bit about him. I knew he was the author of a famous poem called, "The Hound of Heaven." In the poem he pictured God as a hunting hound who was pursuing him down through all the years of his life. He was trying to run away from the Hound of Heaven by finding happiness in other things like his poetry, his art, the beauties of nature, beautiful women he met, and other human beings. At that time I didn't appreciate this part of it—he was a drug addict and he lived on the streets. He was taken in by a very devoted family, the Meynells, and they brought him to a recovery place somewhere in England and he got off the drugs. He lived the rest of his life with this family.

I sat down with his essays and I opened the book at random to an essay that was titled, "Sanity and Sanctity." I devoured that essay. It was fascinating. I didn't realize at the time that Thompson was a recovering, or recovered, drug addict and that by sanity and sanctity, he was saying what we often hear in AA, first you get well and then you get good. Getting well is sanity, health. The health of the body and the mind, of the imagination, of the emotions, and of the will. Like the famous old saying, "A sane mind in a sane body." Sanity means health. It means wholeness, soundness. Everything is there. Nothing that is central is missing. And he pointed out the difference between that and sanctity, which is more religious. Sanctity is the story of a man or a woman in their relationship with God, and how they grow in that relationship. He said they are interdependent and that, as a rule, the healthier a person is, the easier it is for that person to respond to the God of his understanding, to hear his invitations, do his will, and find the profound satisfaction in life in the union with God that will last forever. Some years later, and before I even started to drink, I read another essay by a German Jesuit along the same theme. The title of this essay was, "Holiness is Wholeness." Wholeness is sanity. That's the meaning of the word sanity. It's whole. It's round. Everything is there. Human beings are sane when they are healthy in their bodies and in their minds, in their wills and imaginations. They have an inside light, a way of thinking and feeling and loving that's healthy and whole. This was the same theme, that usually where that wholeness exists, it's easier for a person who is whole to respond to the grace of God, which calls him to a higher level of life that is religious. It's not only spiritual but it's religious.

Although I drank for a number of years, I drank alco-holicly, that is with compulsion for sixteen years. During those years, I gradually deteriorated as a person. I was aware of what was happening, but I didn't understand it. I thought, "If I could only become good, if I could only love God the way I ought to and the way I want to, and if I could be faithful to God's commands and to the obligations of my state of life, then everything would be fine. I never gave up my faith. I always prayed, even when I was drunk. But I was a bender drinker so I had many dry periods and I pleaded with God to straighten me out, to make me a good man and a good priest. But I kept getting worse. This presented a religious difficulty to me. I would wonder why the God of my faith, who I loved so much, was not hearing my prayers. Why wasn't he straightening me out? Instead of getting better, the harder I prayed, the worse I seemed to get.

When I came to the program and I heard at the Twelve Steps and saw the first part of the Twelfth Step—"having had a spiritual awakening as the result of these steps"—my first impulse was to translate that into a religious experience. I thought it meant that having had some kind of a grace-filled experience in a very special encounter with God, I began to do the other things. I was in the program for a few months before I began to realize that the spiritual awakening was what I had read about many years ago. It had to do with my health first.

There is a description of a spiritual awakening in The Twelve and Twelve that appeals to many of us. It does to me. It says by reason of this thing that happens to us called a spiritual awakening, we become able to think and to choose and to do things in a way we weren't able to accomplish before. Basically, that means we get well. We get restored to sanity. That is largely spiritual because we human beings are largely spiritual. We are not just bodies, we are minds and hearts and wills, and we are souls.

It talks about the soul in The Big Book. When I saw that it immediately solved my religious difficulties—"Why doesn't the God of my understanding straighten me out?" And I saw that my religion is a gift of God that is designed to help me to get to heaven—to serve God well in this life and to get to heaven. It's not a medicine. It's not a therapy, a principle that was given to me to get well. I saw that the Twelve Steps of the AA program is a God-given gift. We used to hear that so often, "A God-given program." It is a natural therapy.

Do these things. Rely on God because you can't do anything without him, but rely on him first of all to get well. Rely on him to keep you away from the first drink and to save you from alcoholic thinking. Rely on him to save you from alcoholic emotions, negative emotions, and tantrums, and to help you get out of the drivers seat. Rely on God to help you to stop blaming him and to learn how to go along with life instead of wrestling with it all the time and trying to change it.

That is my perspective and my experience. It has influenced the way I speak at meetings. It may not be the best one for everyone and it might sound at times that I am belittling, as it were, the religious, spiritual experience, but the truth is that it is the most important thing in my life. But I try not to talk too much at a meeting about that aspect because I know there are many people who are not on the same wavelength. So if I have given anybody the impression that I belittled that kind of experience, I certainly don't mean it that way.

Early in AA, I used to wonder about the relationship of AA to my religion. They're not the same thing. They are related to each other, and they can cooperate, but they are not the same thing. I developed this way of looking at it, "God most, but AA first." First doesn't mean most. It means that I do this first. So I try to live the program first so that I will maintain a reasonable amount of health so that I can live in my relationship with God. I'm a priest. It's the most important thing in my life. I want to live that relationship with the God of my faith and of my hope and of my love. That's what I'm about.

I have learned, from various sources—"Sanity and Sanctity," "Holiness is Wholeness," the approach of Alcoholics Anonymous, and these specific steps—that the idea in every one of the Twelve Steps is, first of all, to do something that will protect or improve or maintain my sobriety.

That will get me to a healthy starting point that will enable me to go much further. In the Twelfth Step, two actions are suggested, and both of them are controlled by the same verb "we tried" to carry this message to alcoholics, and "we tried" to practice these principles in all our affairs. Two very important words, "we tried" to do it.

At Guest House, Austin Ripley told us that there have been many movements in our country dealing with alcoholism. There have been temperance movements by many preachers, some of them very powerful preachers. He mentioned a priest Father Matthews. He was either an Irish or an English priest, I don't know which. He was a temperance preacher who didn't understand the nature of the disease as we do. But he was such a powerful preacher that hundreds of suffering alcoholics would stop drinking. But they didn't stay stopped because they didn't have a program to support and maintain their sobriety. Most of them eventually went back to drinking.

This step, like the others, is God-given. We have heard the story so often, when Bill W., with some months of sobriety, went out to Ohio on a business trip. A business deal fell through and he began to get a little fearful about his sobriety. He got the idea that it would help if he could talk with another alcoholic. He got in touch with a local Protestant minister who referred him to Dr. Bob Smith. And Bill went and talked with Bob, and he discovered that an alcoholic who has done something about his problem is very powerful, as a rule, at getting through to another alcoholic. He's talking on the basis of experience—not just scientific learning that he got out of a book—but from his own gut, his own experience. So in this providential way Bill and Bob discovered that one of the best ways to maintain their sobriety was by trying to share it with another alcoholic who is still suffering. To me, that was a God-given insight and light. The point is that in order to maintain our own sobriety and to grow in it, we try to share it with other alcoholics.

There are many, many different ways in which that is done. I remember Father Jim, God rest him, a fellow Jesuit and a close friend, and beloved to many of you. He was such a help to so many of us, including me.

In the early days, Dr. Morrison introduced a four-bed ward for alcoholics at St. Vincent hospital. Father Jim and I used to drop in there and talk with people. One day, when we both dropped in, Jim went to talk to a man who was lying in a bed near the window. There was another man in a bed behind him. Jim talked to the man near the window earnestly. He tried for a couple of hours to give the program to this fellow, but the man didn't buy anything he said. Jim didn't know it, but the man who was lying in the bed behind him listened intently to everything he said. And that man came into the program! The last time I saw him he was over twenty years sober.

We can often carry the message unconsciously by our own sobriety and our own willingness and eagerness to share it unselfishly. Other people see that. Something like this happens at meetings. We might sit at a meeting and think that we are not very active in Twelfth Step work. But when we come to the meeting and sit down, we are saying by our presence that we are alcoholics. We're admitting that we're alcoholics and that we need help. That's why we come to meetings and that's why we listen.

I used to notice old-timers at meeting after meeting after meeting. Their very presence was an eloquent statement. It said, "I'm here because I need it. I want to be sober. I'm willing to be here and to pay this price."

Then we go beyond that in so many different ways. When the right moment arrives, we talk with a sick and suffering alcoholic and share our experience. The Twelfth Step begins by referring to our spiritual awakening and then talks about carrying this message. Does that mean we should reach that degree of recovery in the program before we begin to carry the message? I don't think so. I think we begin right away in small ways or great ways. It's really God who's in charge of the whole thing. He can use any one of us. He has to be there. We don't carry the message. We don't make another person accept it. We generously share with this person, if he wants to listen, what happened to us and how things are now. I think that many people in AA, including me, would say that most of the people that we've talked with over the years and tried to tell the message never bought it. We're only a minority.

Nowadays, we have alcoholics and we have the drug addicts. You hardly ever meet a person who is only an alcoholic. So often it's been a mixture, but basically it's the same thing. It's addiction.

I might try to carry the message to a number of people, most of whom are not ready or don't want to hear it. Or maybe they hear it five or ten years later. In the beginning we might tend to be discouraged. We try to carry the message to people who don't get it, so we think there must be something wrong with us. We alcoholics are prone to think that way. We're guilty before anything happens.

We need to see that it's God who is going to determine whether the person I talk with gets the message, not me. My job, for my own well being and the maintenance of my own sobriety, is to try to give it.

If the person doesn't accept the message right now don't blame yourself, and if he does accept it don't pat yourself on the back and say, "Wow, what a world-beater I am." But it's all right to be grateful and to be happy for this fellow.

So first of all it's for me, but secondly it's for the other person too. And we are so happy to see another suffering alcoholic or an addict get the message and begin to get his or her feet planted on this road to a happy recovery.

We try to carry "this" message. It's not my message. It's the message of the Twelve Steps.

When I was about five months in the program, I was asked to speak at an open meeting in Detroit. Up to this point I had been going to step discussion meetings. I spoke when it came around to me. So I wasn't a person who didn't speak, but this was the first time I spoke at the kind of a meeting that we have around this area. Before I went to the meeting, I asked Ripley if it was all right for me to speak at the meeting since I hadn't done my Fifth Step yet. I wanted to know if I had a right to go down there and talk. He asked me if I intended to do the Fifth Step. When I said that I did, he told me to go to the meeting and talk.

I don't think we have to wait until we've completed the whole program and got it all wrapped up before we carry the message. But I think that the more experience we have with the program and the way it works, the more powerfully we can speak to another alcoholic, because we're speaking out of our experience.

One time at Austin Street, there was a young fellow who came in and he seemed to want somebody to talk to him. So I talked to him for about three quarters of an hour. I was tired but I did my best. When we were finished he looked up at me and he reached out and he snapped my Roman Collar, like this with his fingernail, and he said to me, "Your collar is dirty!"

Now that's what we get sometimes from trying to help a sick and suffering person. They're in a mean mood and they have negative emotions. They're sick. They're not going to respond to us with gratitude or even common ordinary courtesy. When we set out to do Twelfth Step work we've got to be ready for that. If we start too soon or if we get into situations that are too trying for us, it could be very dangerous.

I remember another negative example. There was an old-timer at Austin Street, Bill J., God rest him, a wonderful man who was very, very generous. What a power of example. At Austin Street there was a meeting room and a club room and there was a little kitchen where you could get your coffee. One day a fellow in his early twenties came in. He was a big, tall kid and he wanted to talk. Bill talked to this kid for three solid hours and when he was finished, the kid stood up and raised his arms and yawned and said, "I think I'll go downstairs and have a beer."

That was after three whole hours. But Bill didn't think that he had wasted his time because this fellow went down and had a beer. That would be wrong thinking. We carry the message first of all to help ourselves. We are told so often about our self-centeredness. We get out of ourselves by being willing to share and to carry the message. When we try to help someone, the person might not show any gratitude or appreciation, but on the contrary, he might even insult us. At times it's hard to keep our temper. It's hard to remember that this person is a sick person.

In the beginning, especially when I'm still learning that I'm sick, I can still be in that stage where I think everybody else is doing it on purpose. "I'm sick, but you, you so and so, you're doing it on purpose." It takes a little time to get around to this deeper realization that the other person is sick too.

One day I came into Austin Street and there was a little old-timer there named Tom. He had a gravelly voice and you could hear him a mile away. As I was coming up the stairs I could hear him yelling out, "I have had one hundred percent success with my Twelfth Step work." I thought to myself that Tom was displaying his ego. But I didn't understand. He explained it by saying, "I haven't had a drink. Of these fellows that I tried to help, a few have got the program. Most of them didn't, but I haven't had a drink."

It has its dangers. There used to be a warning, don't go on a Twelfth Step call alone.

I won't stay any longer on that. I'll move on to the next part. "We tried to practice these principles in all our affairs." Generally, I'm sure you will agree, this is the hardest part of the program. It's one thing to try and practice these principles when I'm with fellow alcoholics who are recovering because I know they have some understanding. It's another thing when I'm with other people in my daily life who either are not alcoholics or they are alcoholics who don't admit it. Then it can be awfully hard to practice these principles in all our affairs.

I've often asked myself in the program, what are these principles? We tried—it doesn't say we were completely successful—but we tried to do it. I think the principles are embodied in the steps and in the slogans and in the Serenity Prayer. We are not in the program very long before we learn that we are powerless over alcohol and drugs. Then after a while, we begin to see that we are powerless over other people. That's a revelation. It was to me. While I should have known, I didn't know it in a practical way. I have to accept the fact that I can't change this man or woman. I can't get through to them. I can try to tell them what I think or how I feel or what I desire, but I can't make them agree with me. I have no real power over this person—a sick person perhaps or a well person. I don't have power over other people.

I have to learn how to be a member of the human race. We go back to that sentence, "The alcoholic needs to be restored to the human race." I need to admit and accept my powerlessness over this person. This person may be a relative, a son or a daughter, a brother. I may feel that because I'm his brother, or his father or his mother, that I ought to be able to straighten him out.

Then there's this miserable thing that afflicts us at times, "What are the neighbors going to say about me?" "Just look at her. She can't take care of her own child. What kind of a family is that." When we hear this, it's important that we realize that it's coming from people who don't have the slightest degree of understanding of the real situation. But it's an obstacle for us to learn how to accept that what other people may think about us doesn't change us. That has to do with what's in their head, it doesn't change us, unless we let it get to us and get us troubled and unhappy and miserable.

So there is the principle of my powerlessness over other people and the extension of that principle of powerlessness to certain situations in my life. Why should I spend the whole day grinding my teeth about the weather because it's raining? That's sick isn't it? So apply this principle—I don't have any power over the world. I used to try praying when I wanted to play golf, so I would stand at the window pushing a line up. I was only about forty-five years old! And here I am trying to stop it from raining so I can go play golf. It's as though someone with set purpose said, "We'll get that guy today, I'll make it rain on him and he won't be able to play golf." Self-centeredness. That's just an example. There are many, many different things I'm powerless over. I can accept my powerlessness or I can be a booze fighter, not only with booze or with drugs, but with people, with situations, with the weather, with the state of my health, et cetera. I can stay miserable if I want to, trying to change things I can't change.

Next there are the principles in the Second Step. I guess the main principle is reliance. There's a golden sentence in the Second Chapter in The Twelve and Twelve which says that "What we need is a faith that relies." That's a combination of believing and hoping and trusting. If we believe in this Higher Power, why don't we follow through and lean on him, rely on him. Let him work in my life. Let him do things for me that I can't do for myself. "Help me Lord." I think the Second Step is the asking step, "Help me Lord to accept my powerlessness over this person, over this situation, over these different things in my life. Help me to accept, because without your help, I'll remain sick. I will remain the little child futilely trying to make the world in my own image, to fashion it to my own liking." That's a big one—relying on a Higher Power.

Then, of course, there are the principles in turning my will and my life over to the care of God, of realizing how much, as an addict and alcoholic, I tend to want to run the show. How difficult it is for me to get out of the drivers seat and let a Higher Power be my boss and do my best to cooperate with him, instead of working in place of him or going ahead of him—to let him lead and let me work with him.

In the inventory steps, there is the principle of looking at myself, not in order to find extra reasons for bashing myself, but in order to find out who I am and what are the things in me that need to be changed. What are the strong things that I can work on and make even stronger with God's grace? It's a self-discovery. It's not carried to an extreme, where I spend twenty-four hours a day burrowing into my own personality. I don't think that's recovery. A reasonable knowledge of these things in my life that can be changed, will make life so much better.

In the last two steps, there is the principle of prayer. First of all prayer is a means of getting sane. In addition to that, it's a means of achieving real goodness—spiritual, religious, God-like goodness—that I'm attracted to or that I want to pursue.

In the second or third part of the Eleventh Step we pray only for knowledge of his will for us and the power to carry it out. This is really what grace is. It's a gift from God that's a light in the mind. It throws a light in my path and shows me the way to go, and it is a constant aid to my will which may be weakened or injured. It gives me the power to go ahead and do what I seek to achieve. It lets me step out, put one foot ahead of the other and move.

Then there are the principles in the step that we're talking about, the Twelfth Step. These are the principles of sharing and the effort of practicing these principles in our daily life and in our family. How hard that must be. How hard it is in a community like I live in. How hard it is for all of us. But it's a road that leads to greater and greater health and—God willing and ourselves willing—to a greater degree of goodness and happiness.

There is also the principle of expressing our gratitude—being grateful. We have heard that familiar saying, "You can't be hateful if you're grateful." We discover that gratitude and the expression of gratitude is not only virtuous and pleasing to God, but it is wonderful medicine for a sick alcoholic. The practice of making a gratitude list can be so helpful. We sit down for a few minutes with a piece of paper and a pencil and jot down something we are grateful for. I used to sit down and write, "I'm sober." Then I would pause and meditate a bit and think of all the years when I wasn't sober, when I was in despair, when I was terrified and wondered if I would ever get on my feet again. Then I would think that here I am today, I'm sober. And whether I felt gratitude or not, I would look up to heaven and say, "Thank you, Lord." Even if I didn't feel it, I would say the words. Then I would write, "I have a program," and I would pause and think of all the years when I had no direction with my disease of alcoholism. I didn't even know that I had it. Now I have this wonderful, simple program, guiding my steps. It's a guide. It shows me the way. I would think of the wilderness that I had been in. And I would look up and say, "Thank you, Lord." Then I would write down, "I have a fellowship. I have AA. I have a group of people who are like me in this area." We don't have to draw maps for each other. We know from the inside what this damnable disease feels like. No matter what station in life we come from, there are not special kinds of alcoholism. There are different states of life, but it's all the same damnable disease. We know one another, even though we don't know each other's names at times. If we're alcoholics, we're fellow sufferers, and we're fellows in recovery.

Writing a few things down like that and saying thank you is wonderful medicine. I find that, although in the beginning I might not have felt much like saying "thank you," by the time I get down to the end I'm probably saying it and meaning it. It's coming from my heart, "Thank you, thank you." Again, this is a principle of action. It's doing something, not waiting until we feel like doing it. And we do it over and over and after awhile we probably feel like doing it. We have all heard people in AA say, "I came to AA meetings until I wanted to come." We know what that means. We came at first because it seemed the right thing to do, or we were told to come, or we were forced to come. But we kept coming. We did the action. By performing the action something wonderful got through to us, and now we want to come to meetings.

What an awakening that is. It is the principle of action and it's used in Recovery Incorporated, which is another program. People who are bogged down with emotional problems, fears of one kind or another, share with each other this way—they encourage each other to do something. For example, a person is afraid to leave the house. They encourage the person to get his hat and his coat and just walk down to the corner. If that's all the person can do, they are urged to do that. They are urged to take action. Action is the magic word. So the expression of gratitude is an action. Many of us don't naturally gravitate towards expressing gratitude because we're so awfully self-centered and self-willed. But once again, Ripley used to say, "If you can't be grateful, you can't recover." The principle of gratitude can be wonderful medicine for all of us and we can choose to use it even when we don't feel like it. If I say, "I'll wait till tomorrow, maybe I'll feel like it tomorrow." Maybe I won't. Maybe I'll go the rest of my life without feeling like it. It's like taking the bull by the horns—do it. Say the words, write it down, go through the motions and keep doing it, and after awhile it will come alive and you'll be glad to do it.

In the Twelfth Step, in The Twelve and Twelve, it has a beautiful paragraph that I should have memorized but I haven't. But I think you'll recall it. It enumerates the things that we are able to do through this program, the things that ordinary healthy people can do with their lives. We can go to work regularly. We can pay our bills. We can cooperate with our fellow workers. And there are about six or seven other things like that. It's a wonderful paragraph. It's like the promises—that we can be restored to health and sanity through this program. Having been restored to sanity, if we hear the voice of the God of our understanding, the way is open and we can find in our lives a friendship with our God. So I'm very grateful for you all being here and listening and I hope sincerely that each one of you will be given the best of God's gift and the best kind of sobriety, so that every day of your life will be a day of growing health, growing happiness, and gratitude and friendship with the Lord. Thank you all.

*              *              *

We have come to the end of our gatherings, but before we say the Lord's Prayer, I want to add a couple of words. The Big Book says it doesn't make any difference who we meet in AA as long as we trust in God and clean house. But I know that my life and your life and the lives of hundreds and hundreds and hundreds and hundreds of people who aren't here tonight have been enriched by the fact that Father Fred is a member of our fellowship. He is a very special person, and God has given him to us and blessed us in certain qualities and certain experiences that he has—his priesthood, his rigorous training in the Society of Jesus, his gift of counsel, his gift of wisdom, his gift of humility. So I want to say to Father Fred, "Thank you," but I especially want to say to God, "Thank you for placing Father Fred on our Happy Road of Destiny."

Ambassador Books, Inc.

*also publishes*

# The Anonymous Disciple

by

**Gerard E. Goggins**

a novel based on the lives of

Father Jim and Father Fred